MW00678862

flower *arranging*

STEP-BY-STEP INSTRUCTIONS FOR EVERYDAY DESIGNS

TERESA P. LANKER   PHOTOGRAPHY BY STEPHEN SMITH

florists'review

President: Travis Rigby

Photographer: Stephen Smith

© 2007, 2008, 2010, 2012, 2013, 2014, 2015, 2016 WildFlower Media Inc. All Rights Reserved. No part of this publication may be reproduced without prior written permission of the publisher.

Flower Arranging: Step-by-Step Instructions for Everyday Designs is produced by WildFlower Media Inc. Topeka, Kansas. *www.floristsreview.com*

Design and typesetting by WildFlower Media Inc.; Topeka, Kansas.

Printed in China

ISBN: 978-0-9714860-8-9

Some products courtesy of:
Smithers-Oasis Company, *www.oasisfloral.com*
Pioneer Balloon Company, *www.qualatex.com*

Florists' Review is the only independent trade magazine for professional florists in the United States. In addition to serving the needs of retail florists through its monthly publication, *Florists' Review* has an active book division that supplies educational products to all who are interested in floral design. For more information, visit *www.floristsreview.com* or call (800) 367-4708.

Contents

Introduction 5

I Getting Started 6
- 7 Mixing flower food
- 7 Soaking floral foam
- 8 Cutting floral foam
- 8 Securing floral foam
- 9 Using chicken wire
- 10 Preparing vases
- 11 Greening containers
- 15 Adding accessories

II Everyday Designs 18
- 19 One-sided triangle
- 23 Round centerpiece
- 27 Oblong centerpiece
- 31 One dozen roses in a vase

III Flowers to Wear 36
- 37 Wiring and taping
- 42 Wiring chart
- 44 Making bows
- 49 Designing a boutonniere
- 51 Designing a corsage
- 55 Designing a wrist corsage
- 58 Designing hair flowers

IV Sympathy Arrangements 62
- 63 Traditional sympathy basket
- 67 Casket spray
- 73 Easel spray
- 77 Sympathy wreath
- 80 Sympathy tribute forms
- 81 Sympathy cross
- 84 Set pieces
- 85 10 tips for working with funeral directors

V Wedding Bouquets 86
- 87 Round bouquet
- 91 Cascade bouquet
- 95 Hand-tied bouquet
- 99 Securing stems
- 102 Adding accessories to bouquets
- 104 Bouquet backings
- 107 Bouquet handles

VI Balloons 112
- 114 Safety and environmental issues
- 115 Inflation and sealing
- 118 Special balloon treatments
- 120 Balloon bouquets
- 121 Balloon accessories

VII Displays 122
- 123 Floral display types
- 123 Display elements
- 128 Display principles
- 132 Planning a display calendar
- 133 Display checklist

VIII Packaging 134
- 135 Weather conditions
- 136 Wrapping loose stems and bouquets
- 141 Packaging loose flowers in boxes
- 143 Wrapping arrangements
- 145 Packaging corsages and boutonnieres
- 147 Wrapping plants
- 150 Wrapping gift baskets

Care and Handling 152
Flower Glossary 153-156
Foliage Glossary 157
Index 158
Bibliography 159

TERESA P. LANKER

Teresa Lanker is assistant professor and coordinator of Floral Design and Marketing at The Ohio State University Agricultural Technical Institute, in Wooster, Ohio, a position she has held since 1986. She also serves as chair of the Horticultural Technologies Division.

In addition to her administrative and teaching duties at OSU, Teresa is responsible for the operation of the university flower shop, and she advises the campus *Artistes de Fleur* floral design club as well as the Anderson Student Chapter of the American Institute of Floral Designers (AIFD).

Teresa holds a bachelor of science degree in Ornamental Horticulture and a master of education degree, both from the University of Illinois. In addition, she is credentialed by the American Floral Art School in Chicago.

Since 1999, Teresa has written a monthly column for *Florists' Review* magazine. Additionally, she contributed to the *Encycloflora* textbooks published by Teleflora / Redbook Florist Services, *Florists' Review*'s *A Centennial History of the American Florist* and educational materials for The Ohio State University Curriculum Materials Service. Teresa also has been a featured designer in *Florists' Review, Florists' Review Weddings* and *Florists' Review Christmas* as well as wire-service selection guides.

A presenter of design seminars and workshops throughout the United States, Teresa also has been actively involved with the Ohio Florists' Association and its annual Short Course for many years. She has served on the educational design teams for Teleflora and Redbook Florist Services as well as Redbook's Educational Advisory Board.

When not teaching, writing or traveling to floral industry events, Teresa enjoys spending time with her husband and four children. Together they share interests in gardening, cycling and spending time at the beach.

Introduction

Flower arranging is a skill and an art. For some, floral design is a hobby, passion or source of relaxation. For others, it is a career that provides them the opportunity to earn a living while communing daily with nature. Learning to design flowers can be accomplished through trial and error, but developing design expertise is faster and easier when guided by established methods and examples.

This book is intended to assist the aspiring floral designer in advancing his or her skills, with detailed step-by-step instructions for designs of all kinds. From everyday arrangements to wedding bouquets to sympathy designs, the classic design shapes and styles are demonstrated with thorough text and photographs. For each illustrated design, variations are provided, showing creative alternatives for designers to try as their skills advance.

As with any form of art, there are many different ways to approach the design of flowers. The methods used in this book represent those that have proved especially successful among floral design students with little or no prior design experience. While the bulk of this book focuses on flower arranging, a number of supporting topics, such as design mechanics, balloon basics, display and packaging, are included to help broaden the designer's understanding of how arrangements might be accessorized, wrapped and showcased to best advantage. A comprehensive flower glossary and accompanying care-and-handling appendix provide the information needed to select and condition flowers for optimal use.

Like the loveliest of flower arrangements, this book has been carefully designed to make reading and learning about flowers a pleasure. Whether you are a floral design novice, a hobbyist, a well-seasoned apprentice or a professional, this book offers the information and illustrations you need to advance. Take the lessons at your own pace, and enjoy the process of growing into an accomplished floral designer.

GETTING STARTED

Before a single flower is placed in an arrangement, there are a variety of preparatory steps that may be necessary to get the design process under way. Each design situation has its own set of requirements. Sometimes, such as with a bouquet of flowers in a vase, minimal mechanics are needed. Conversely, some arrangements, such as funeral designs, require multiple mechanical techniques to be employed prior to creation.

The following techniques provide a sampling of the procedures and mechanics used frequently in preparation for designing a variety of arrangement types.

MIXING FLOWER FOOD

A number of different flower food (or "preservative") brands are available for use in extending fresh flower longevity. Most of these "foods" have a common formulation, consisting of sugar, citric acid and bactericide. When mixed properly, following label directions, they have the capability of extending flower life by a few to several days.

When mixing flower food, be sure to use clean containers and warm water, and be sure to stir well to properly dissolve all ingredients. For the purpose of **bud opening**, most flower foods can be mixed at twice the regular rate until the buds have opened to the degree desired. At that time, the flowers should be placed into a solution of water and flower food mixed at the regular rate.

A properly mixed flower-food solution should be used not only in flower storage containers but also in design bowls and vases. Floral foam should be soaked in water that has been properly mixed with flower food. And customers should be given packets of flower food for home use as well.

Flower foods have been formulated to provide the proper balance of ingredients, so it is best to **follow label directions** and avoid homemade flower-food formulations.

Figure 1-1. Soaking floral foam.

SOAKING FLORAL FOAM

Floral foam always should be allowed to **float freely** in a container of flower-food solution that is larger than the size of the foam block. Ideally, the water level in the container should be at least twice the depth of the foam to be soaked (Figure 1-1). A single standard-sized block of floral foam (approximately 9 inches x 4 inches x 3 inches) holds about two quarts of water. As the foam absorbs water, it will sink. A fully soaked block of foam will be completely submerged within about one to two minutes, with no sign of air bubbles rising from it (Figure 1-2).

For best results, **never force floral foam under water** in an attempt to hasten water absorption. Doing so will result in the development of air pockets inside the block. Flower stems inserted into these dry areas of the foam will have no water source.

Figure 1-2. Submerged floral foam.

Figure 1-3. Foam extending above the container.

Figure 1-4. Inserting foam vertically.

In most cases, floral foam should be cut to a size that will fit snugly in the selected container. For some design styles, however, it may be desirable to fill only a portion of a bowl, saucer or design tray. In either case, the foam will need to extend about ½ inch to 1 inch above the container edge to allow for horizontal stem insertions (Figure 1-3). (Note: For some contemporary design styles, there is a trend toward keeping the foam at or below the container edge.)

In the case of an **upright (vertical) container**, a block of foam can be turned on end and trimmed to fit, or foam scraps can be placed in the lower portion of the container to support a block of foam in the top (Figure 1-4). It is not advisable to wedge a block of foam into the top of a container without adding supporting foam beneath it because the foam may change shape during the design process and fall into the container.

Some designers find it helpful to **bevel the edges** of the floral foam in a container to create more surface areas for angled stem insertions. This can be done prior to designing by slicing off the straight corners on each side of the block with a floral knife or foam-cutting knife (Figure 1-5).

To enable the customer to replace water in a container filled with floral foam, create a **water well.** To do this, simply cut out a small notch in the foam in the back of the container, removing a section of foam the full depth of the block. Be sure to keep the water well clear of flowers and foliage so that the customer can access the space with a pitcher or watering can (Figure 1-6).

Figure 1-5. Beveling foam edges.

Figure 1-6. Creating a water well.

Figure 1-7. Securing foam with waterproof tape.

To prevent floral foam from shifting in containers, it is typically secured with tape, glue or other mechanics. **Waterproof tape,** available in ¼-inch and ½-inch widths, can be crisscrossed over the foam, anchoring the tape ends to the edges of the container (Figure 1-7). For small to medium arrangements, ¼-inch tape is sufficient. For larger designs, ½-inch tape is useful. When taping the foam, avoid creating an "X" (or intersection) directly in the center of the container where it could interfere with central flower insertions. If the tape ends don't adhere well, additional tape can be placed around the rim of the container to secure them.

Hot-melt glue is another option for securing foam into a container. Either a low-temp glue gun or glue pan can be used, though the glue pan is generally easier to use and provides better coverage (Figure 1-8). It is important to start with dry floral foam that has been cut to the desired size. Dip one side of the foam block into the pan of melted glue, and press the foam into position in the container. Allow the glue to harden for a few seconds, then immerse the foam-filled container into a tub, bucket or sink filled with flower-food solution, allowing it to float freely until the foam is completely soaked.

Figure 1-8. Securing floral foam with glue.

Anchor pins provide an easy means of securing floral foam into containers, especially for situations where there is a need to fill only a portion of a container with foam. These small, four-pronged, plastic aids can be used singly for small pieces of foam or in multiples for securing larger blocks. They can be attached to the bottom of the container (prongs facing up) with hot-melt glue from either a

glue gun or glue pan. Once the glue sets, the foam is simply pressed onto the anchor pins until it rests against the bottom of the container, hiding the pins (Figure 1-9).

Baskets or other containers with liners sometimes require an additional step to adequately secure both the foam to the liner and the liner to the container. Usually, the foam can be secured to the liner with either hot-melt glue or waterproof tape. However, glue is frequently not an option for securing a liner to a basket or other nonsolid container surface. Waterproof tape can be used for some containers but may not adhere well to the irregular surfaces of many baskets. For a handled basket, a thick rubber band slid down over the handle works well to hold the foam-filled liner in place (Figure 1-10). For a basket without a handle, waxed string can be placed in the basket beneath the liner, with the ends pulled up opposite sides and through the basket weave near the rim of the basket. The ends then can be tied over the top of the foam-filled liner.

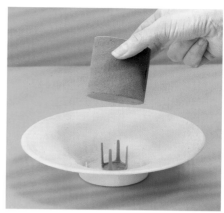

Figure 1-9. Securing foam with anchor pins.

Figure 1-10. Securing foam in baskets.

USING CHICKEN WIRE

For some flower arrangements, especially large ones such as sympathy or altar arrangements, it is desirable to provide **added support** to the floral foam. Chicken wire is frequently used for this purpose. To do so, cut a piece of chicken wire slightly larger than the foam surface to be covered. Push the ends of one side of the chicken wire into the foam on one side of the block. Bend the wire across the foam surface, and push the other ends into the opposite side of the foam block. Secure the chicken wire to the container with crisscrossed pieces of waterproof tape (Figure 1-11).

Alternatives to chicken wire include waterproof tape, strapped several times in each direction over a large foam foundation, or a foam-filled cage, in which a plastic cage surrounds and supports the foam within. In addition, floral foam can

be wrapped in florist foil not only to provide support but also to help retain moisture within the foam.

Figure 1-11. Chicken wire reinforcing foam.

Figure 1-12. Creating a grid with tape.

Figure 1-13. Hiding floral foam with leaves.

There are a variety of ways to prepare vases prior to arranging flowers within. The simplest preparation, preferred by many experienced designers, is to fill the vase with flower-food solution, then arrange flowers. However, sometimes the flowers need support in order to achieve a desired shape or style, especially when the selected vase is large.

Grids can be used to narrow the space within which each stem is placed, which helps to control the positions of the flowers within an arrangement. Ready-made plastic grids, usually white or clear, are available from floral product suppliers in an assortment of sizes to fit over the top of standard-sized vases. Waterproof tape or clear tape, such as *Oasis® Clear Tape*, can be used to make custom grids, crisscrossing as many strips of tape as desired over the mouth of the vase (Figure 1-12). Chicken wire also can be used as a grid, with a well-trimmed piece taped over the container opening.

Foam products can be used in several ways to provide stem support in vases. For opaque containers, standard floral foam can be used in a similar manner to other types of containers. For transparent vases, however, it is not desirable to see any form of mechanics inside the vase; therefore, standard floral foam generally should not be used unless it is hidden by other decorative items, such as fresh leaves on the inside or outside of the glass (Figure 1-13).

Shredded plastic foam, once popular as a vase arrangement mechanic, has been joined by **colored foams** available in powder and blocks. These foams provide not only support but also an added decorative effect to vases. Powdered foam should be poured into the vase while dry, with water added slowly until the foam is adequately moistened but not so wet that it floats. Colored foam blocks should be soaked before use. They can be cut into small cubes or scooped into "melon" balls to create an interesting textural effect inside the vase (Figure 1-14).

Decorative **marbles** or **pebbles** are another type of mechanical aid for vases. A shallow layer or several inches of marbles or pebbles can be placed into the bottom of any transparent vase to add interest as well as flower support (Figure 1-15). A deep layer provides more support but may make stem insertions more difficult. Use caution when placing marbles or pebbles into glass vases in order to prevent the vases from breaking.

Figure 1-14. Colored foams.

Figure 1-15. Decorative marbles or pebbles.

GREENING CONTAINERS

The process of preparing a container with foliage prior to arranging the flowers is commonly known as "greening." Greening the container serves a variety of purposes. It establishes the basic outline or silhouette of the arrangement, softens the appearance of flower stems, provides transition at the container edge, covers mechanics and provides a background of greenery to set off the flowers.

Generally, the foliage framework created during the greening process should be slightly smaller than the finished flower arrangement. This prevents the design from being dominated by greens. However, for some arrangements, it may be desirable to create a foliage framework that extends beyond the flowers, and for others, it may be desirable to minimize the appearance of foliage altogether. Typically, one to three types of foliage are used during the greening process, with any additional desired foliage incorporated as filler after the flowers. There are numerous ways to green a container. Some examples follow.

Traditional Greening for One-Sided Arrangements

The steps that follow are for greening a one-sided arrangement in a triangular shape. This process can be modified easily for other one-sided design shapes by changing stem lengths and positions.

Establish a central vertical axis by placing a piece of foliage centered near the back edge of the container. The height of this stem should be slightly lower than the desired finished design height. (Finished design height should be approximately 1½ - 2 times the height of the container.) The angle of the stem should be slightly backward rather than perfectly upright.

Extend a stem of foliage out from each side of the container to a length that, in proportion to the height placement, forms the desired design shape. Make sure both stems are equal in length and perfectly horizontal once positioned, facing upward (rather than forward).

Place one or two stems of foliage horizontally at the front lip of the container, again facing upward, to define the depth of the design. Insert these stems at a length that, from a side view, provides a gentle slope from their tips to the tip of the vertical piece of foliage.

Add more stems of foliage horizontally at the lip of the container to fill in between the side stems and the center stems. Allow each insertion to slightly overlap the stem(s) beside it. All of these placements should rest against the container edge and should face upward.

Add stems of foliage between the tip of the vertical piece of foliage and the side placements to create the sides of the triangle. These stems should be angled backward slightly. The front side of the foliage should face forward.

Position two stems of foliage into the center of the container so that they face each other and arch outward toward the sides of the design. Be sure the lengths of these stems do not reach beyond the established foliage framework.

Continue adding foliage, as needed, into the center of the design following a natural radiating pattern from the middle outward. Be sure all stems remain within the boundaries of the design outline.

Turn the container around, and cover the container edge and any visible mechanics in the back of the container with foliage scraps.

Traditional Greening for All-Around Arrangements

The following steps are for greening a round or circular arrangement. This process can be modified easily for other all-around design shapes by changing stem lengths and positions.

Position three stems of foliage into the center of the container so that they face each other and arch away from center in a somewhat fountainlike manner. The lengths of all these stems should be the same and should establish a central design height that is nearly 1½ - 2 times the height of the container.

Arrange additional tips of foliage horizontally and facing upward around the edge of the container in a slightly overlapping manner. Visualize the desired all-around design shape, whether a low dome, an upright mound or something in between, and be sure these foliage tips extend to the length necessary (in proportion to the central foliage stems) to achieve it. The lengths of all these stems should be the same.

Add more foliage stems between the center insertions and the horizontal insertions in a radiating manner so that all of the foliage appears to "sprout" from the center outward. Use enough foliage to establish a complete shape and cover most mechanics. When fern foliage is used, for example, the result should look like a small fern plant.

Greening Before and After

In some situations, it may be preferable not to use very much foliage during the greening process in order to leave plenty of space in the foam for large- or soft-stemmed flower insertions. In this case, a minimal amount of foliage can be used to define the design shape, with additional foliage added after the flowers are arranged to cover mechanics and soften the appearance of stems.

Mossing

This method of container preparation utilizes moss, usually sheet moss or Spanish moss, in place of (or sometimes in addition to) foliage to cover the floral foam and mechanics. When using sheet moss, moisten the moss, squeeze out any excess water, then pull the moss to create an open mesh and place this thin layer over the foam (Figure 1-16). When using Spanish moss, a minimal layer is best. If either type of moss is applied too thickly, it may be necessary to pierce the moss with a knife in order to insert flower stems through it.

Figure 1-16. Concealing foam with sheet moss.

Collaring

Collaring is a basic greening technique sometimes used for round arrangements, centerpieces and bouquets. It involves arranging foliage around the edge of the container only (Figure 1-17). Often, this is done with one of many types of broadleaf foliages, such as *Galax,* salal or *Magnolia,* but any type of foliage, from feathery plumosa to spiky *Equisetum* to graceful bear grass, can be used depending on the look desired. This technique is especially useful for design styles in which the flower placements are very dense, thus creating a thick mass of flowers over the uncovered foam.

Wrapping

This quick technique can be used when it is not necessary to create a foliage outline of the design shape to come. Typically, fluffy, fillerlike foliage, such as sprengeri fern or plumosa fern, is used. If long pieces are available, often only one stem is needed. Insert the stem end into the side of the foam horizontally, and coil the piece of foliage around the edge using greening pins or small pieces of wire bent into hairpins to secure the foliage in place. Continue wrapping onto the top of the foam and pin the tip down to finish (Figure 1-18).

Lacing

Lacing is a technique used when greening and assembling vase arrangements. It is also the process some designers use to make hand-tied bouquets. Lacing involves creating a network of interwoven stems that support and hold each other in position. The more stems that are added, the more interlocked they become.

To green a vase using the lacing technique, follow the steps below.

Figure 1-17. *Collaring with Galax leaves.*

Figure 1-18. *Wrapping with plumosa fern.*

Arrange five stems of foliage as horizontally as possible to lie against the container edge. The stems should intertwine diagonally with each other.

Arrange three additional stems of foliage upright in the center of the vase making sure the foliages face each other and radiate outward, intertwining with the previously positioned stems. Add more foliage between the top and edge placements.

ADDING ACCESSORIES

Accessories provide added interest to many flower arrangements and allow customers to add token gifts or keepsakes to their flower purchases. Candy, balloons and plush animals are examples of popular accessory options, but customer requests run the gamut from jewelry to currency, lotions to gardening tools, figurines to fruit. Attachment methods vary greatly depending on the item to be added and its placement within a design. Whenever possible, care should be taken to use mechanics that maintain the keepsake value of the accessory (e.g., no glue on plush, no florist clay on lotion bottles). Although many accessory items require one-of-a-kind mechanics, the following techniques are widely used.

Mechanics for Candles

A simple mechanic for adding candles to an arrangement is a plastic **candle adapter**, or **candle stake**. Using these devices, a taper or pillar candle is tightly pressed into the shallow base of the adapter. Beneath the base is a pointed tip or set of prongs that can be inserted into the floral foam until the adapter base rests atop the foam (Figure 1-19). For maximum security, this should be done prior to greening the container.

Figure 1-19. Using candle adapters.

Occasionally, a candle is too thick or too thin to fit into an adapter. If the candle is too thick, the base can be shaved with a floral knife to fit the adapter. If the candle is too thin, waterproof tape can be wrapped around the candle base several times until the required thickness is achieved.

Wood picks, together with waterproof tape, provide a viable alternative to candle adapters. For this mechanic, begin wrapping the base of a pillar or taper candle with ½-inch waterproof tape. Once the tape has encircled the candle one time, add a wood pick and continue taping to secure the pick in place. Continue this process, adding more picks as needed to support the candle. Taper candles usually require only two picks. Pillars may need four or more picks (Figure 1-20). (Note: The length of the picks used should increase as candle height increases. For example, use 3-inch picks for 6-inch to 8-inch tapers; use 4-inch picks for 10-inch to 15-inch tapers; and use 6-inch picks for 18-inch or taller candles.)

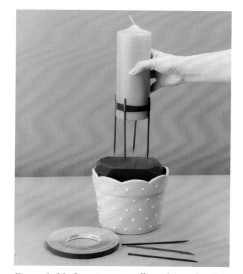

Figure 1-20. Securing a candle with wood picks.

Once picked, the candle can be secured atop the floral foam. The picks should be inserted into the foam so that the candle base touches the foam or is pressed slightly into it. Sometimes candles are inserted into floral foam without the use of picks. When doing so, it is imperative that the candles be sunken deeply into the foam so that they are very secure.

For securing votive candles into arrangements, **anchor pins** are an effective mechanic. Using hot-melt glue or florist clay, simply adhere the base of a votive cup to the top of an anchor pin. Insert the four prongs of the anchor pin into the floral foam until the top of the anchor pin rests atop the foam (Figure 1-21).

Figure 1-21. Securing a votive with anchor pins.

Figure 1-22. Securing plush items.

Mechanics for Plush Items

The mechanics used to secure plush animals or characters into flower arrangements should not mar the accessories in any way. Rather than gluing, taping or piercing devices onto or into plush, the preferred mechanics involve tying one or more ribbons around the neck, waist or legs of the animal and securing the ribbon to one or more hyacinth stakes or cardholders behind the object. The stakes then can be inserted deeply into the floral foam so that the item rests in the desired position within the design. It is best to do this after greening because the foliage will help keep the plush character off the wet foam (Figure 1-22). To further prevent water damage, place colored cellophane or waxed tissue as a decorative barrier between the plush item and the foam.

Mechanics for Ceramic Figures

Ceramic or other breakable accessories can be secured in a similar manner to plush items. Due to the additional weight these items often have, two or more wood picks or hyacinth stakes are typically better choices for stabilizing ceramics than cardholders. Taping or tying the ceramic item to the stakes in more than one place, including an attachment close to the base, is recommended. Long stakes also are necessary so they can be inserted deeply into the floral foam.

For ceramics that have a hole in the base, an alternative attachment method is to position a pair of picks or stakes deep into the floral foam to form a broad "V." The stakes are then carefully pressed close enough together so that the hole in the ceramic object will fit over them. Then the ceramic item can be slid down the stakes into position (Figure 1-23). The resistance provided by the stakes against the interior of the object will provide reliable stability.

Figure 1-23. Securing ceramic figures.

Mechanics for Candy and Other Edibles

Mechanics for edible accessories always should be designed with the assumption that the food eventually will be eaten. Nothing should be done to harm food items inside their packages. **Boxed candy** wrapped in ribbon can be secured to stakes, allowing the box to be perched within a flower arrangement (Figure 1-24). If the box is not wrapped in plastic or cellophane, care should be taken to prevent the box from resting against wet foam.

Individually wrapped candies can be gathered into boutonniere bags or squares of tulle tied with ribbon to wood picks or cardholders (Figure 1-25). Alternatively, a novel look can be achieved by gluing wrapped candies into the centers of flowers, such as Hershey's Kisses™ into the centers of carnations (Figure 1-26). A cool-melt glue gun can be used to secure miniature or full-sized candy bars to wood picks or hyacinth stakes that then can be inserted into vase arrangements or designs created in floral foam.

Fruits and vegetables are sometimes used as natural accents among flowers in arrangements, such as miniature pumpkins in autumn designs. When arranged as design components rather than edible accessories, they sometimes can be inserted directly into the floral foam, such as in the case of asparagus. Larger fruits and vegetables that cannot be inserted into foam require wood picks to secure them. In most cases, two picks inserted directly into the fruits or vegetables are better than one because the pair of picks prevents large or heavy produce from spinning (Figure 1-27).

Figure 1-24. Securing boxed candy.

Figure 1-25. Securing candies onto a wood pick.

Figure 1-26. Gluing individual, wrapped candies into carnations.

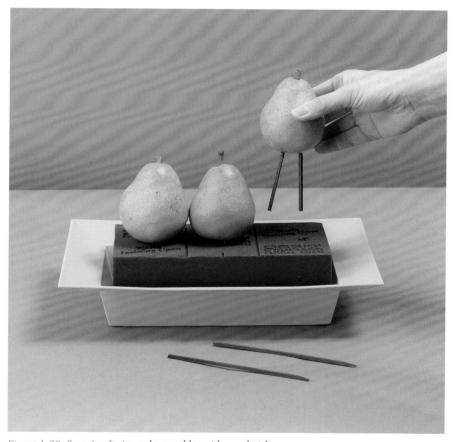

Figure 1-27. Securing fruits and vegetables with wood picks.

II

EVERYDAY DESIGNS

In the day-to-day work of most flower shops, there are a few key design styles that are standard fare. Whether the occasion is a birthday, an anniversary or a new baby, whether the location is a hospital room, a kitchen or an office, the arrangement created is most likely founded in one of these traditional styles. Mastering these everyday arrangements is an important first step toward becoming a creative floral designer. After learning the traditional models of these designs, begin introducing greater style through the suggested variations.

ONE-SIDED TRIANGLE

Floral arrangements in triangular shapes are standard fare in most flower shops. They are used frequently for everyday orders, including flowers for the home, office or hospital. They also are commonly scaled up for use in wedding ceremonies and funerals.

The step-by-step instructions that follow are for the floral industry's mainstay triangular design shape: a symmetrical isosceles triangle with two equal sides and a shorter base. By expanding the baseline to a length equal to the sides, an equilateral variation can be achieved.

Although symmetrical triangles are the most common, asymmetrical types provide the opportunity for greater expression of style and drama. After mastering the traditional triangle illustrated here, try one of the four asymmetrical variations that follow.

SUGGESTED MATERIALS

12 roses
⅓-½ bunch mass flowers, such as spray
  (miniature) carnations
3-4 stems waxflowers
5-6 stems myrtle
3-4 stems leatherleaf fern
2-3 stems oregonia
Design bowl or compote
Floral foam/mechanics

DESIGN STEPS

Prepare the container with floral foam. (See Chapter I, Pages 7-9.)

Place one piece of myrtle to establish a vertical line approximately 1½ - 2 times the height of the container and centered in the back of the foam.

Arrange two more stems of myrtle to establish the side points of the triangle. The length of these pieces of myrtle should be such that the resulting baseline of the triangle is approximately ⅔ the length of the vertical placement. Angle these stems downward slightly.

Arrange three to five smaller tips and side shoots of myrtle radiating around the front edge of the container and connecting the two side points across the baseline. Arrange these stems so they appear to angle from the center of the container outward and slightly downward. The stems front and center in the container should be the longest (2½" - 3").

Arrange additional pieces of myrtle to visually connect the tips of the horizontal and vertical placements and create a triangular outline. Arrange remaining tips of myrtle in the center of the design, radiating outward toward the established edges of the triangle.

Fill in any remaining areas of exposed floral foam with leatherleaf fern, making sure the fern does not extend beyond the established triangular outline. Arrange a rose so that the bloom is at the top of the triangle, just below the tip of the myrtle.

7

Arrange five more roses in a stair-stepped trunk line, placing the flowers closer together as they approach the baseline. The roses should progress from less open at the top to more open at the bottom, and the stem angles should graduate from relatively upright to nearly horizontal.

8

Arrange a rose horizontally on each side of the arrangement at the container edge to define the two low points of the triangle.

9

Arrange the remaining four roses evenly within the triangular outline.

10

Arrange the miniature carnations between the roses, beginning in the focal area and moving up the trunk line and out to the edges of the triangle.

11

Arrange small accent pieces of the oregonia throughout the lower half of the design.

12

Complete the design with the addition of waxflowers or other filler flowers following the same procedure used with the spray carnations. Be sure to distribute the filler flowers evenly, following a radiating stem pattern.

VARIATIONS

I. Classic "L"-Shaped Arrangement with Accessories

The classic "L"-shaped arrangement (a right-angle scalene triangle) is an asymmetrical triangular design that is easy to relate to. Based on the familiar shape of the capital letter "L," this design style is an appropriate choice when an accent or accessory, such as a box of chocolates, plush animal or holiday symbol, is desired (Figure 2-1).

To create an "L"-shaped arrangement, start with a trunk line to the left of center. Add a strong horizontal line to the right, with virtually no line to the left. Be sure the height-to-width proportions are consistent with those of the letter "L." Add a focal point where these two lines merge. Make sure each line broadens slightly as it approaches the focal area, and be sure there is adequate depth among the flower placements so that the design does not appear flat. For added impact, insert an accessory that is proportionate to the design size within the angle of the "L." (See "Adding Accessories," Page 16.)

II. Dramatic Scalene Triangle Arrangement (with Obtuse or Acute Angles)

Obtuse-angle scalene triangles (a "lazy 'L'") and acute-angle scalene triangles (an "A" with unequally angled legs) are characterized by having three unequal sides. These unusual asymmetrical design shapes are good choices when a dramatic statement is desired. Be careful to balance the placements of the initial triangle points, or the resulting design can appear unstable. Strong development of depth from the front of the design to the back (versus a one-dimensional or "flat" design) is also key to establishing the necessary balance for this style (Figure 2-2).

III. Contemporary Triangle with Groupings

To create a triangular design with a modern flair, use flowers and foliages in groups rather than scattered. Minimize the amount of each flower used so that the emphasis is more on lines and flower forms than on mass. Start with the same three placements of the triangle's points, but use a different flower type at each point. Place another one to three flower types in groups within the focal area. Allow strong groupings with interesting variations in flower forms, textures and colors to dominate while the implied triangular silhouette becomes secondary (Figure 2-3).

IV. Church Vases

Often designed in pairs, church vases can be made symmetrical or asymmetrical. Triangular forms are common, including the tall and narrow (vertical) isosceles shape. Asymmetrical alternatives include "L"-shaped (right-angle scalene triangle) as well as obtuse-angle scalene triangle ("lazy 'L'") and acute-angle scalene triangle (an "A" with unequally angled legs) designs. When asymmetrical styles are used in pairs, the two arrangements must be designed as mirror images of each other (Figure 2-4). It is best to design paired arrangements simultaneously, establishing the height of each, then the trunk lines and so on, so that the two designs have a comparable shape and volume.

Church vases typically are designed in plastic or metal liners that fit inside the more decorative vases owned by the church. Although they can be designed in water, they are more commonly prepared using a floral-foam foundation.

Figure 2-1. Classic "L"-shaped arrangement with box of chocolates.

Figure 2-2. Dramatic scalene triangle arrangement with an obtuse angle.

Figure 2-3. Contemporary triangle with groupings.

Figure 2-4. "L"-shaped church vases designed in a mirrored pair.

JILL PREVOST
673 STEEPLE CHASE DR
LAWRENCEVILLE, GA 30044-6026

ROUND CENTERPIECE

The round centerpiece, sometimes referred to as a "roundy moundy," is a standard arrangement shape for situations where the flowers will be viewed from all sides. By definition, the form of the design should be round; however, variations include low, tightly massed styles and open, airy, loosely rounded styles.

SUGGESTED MATERIALS

3-4 stems daisy spray mums (pompons)

4-5 stems spray (miniature) carnations

2-3 stems statice

4-6 stems leatherleaf fern

Round bowl or compote

Floral foam/mechanics

DESIGN STEPS

1

Prepare the container with floral foam. (See Chapter 1, Pages 7-9.)

2

Green the container with leatherleaf fern. (See Chapter 1, Page 13.) Position a single daisy mum in the center of the foam at a height that is 1½ times the width of a low bowl or 1½ times the height of a compote.

3

Position three daisy mums, spaced equidistant from one another, horizontally at the edge of the container. The lengths of all three daisies should be such that once they are inserted into the foam, they create a total design width (diameter) that is no more than the design height.

4

Check the daisy mums from a bird's-eye view. They should appear to form an equilateral triangle. Be sure each daisy mum stem is touching the container edge and has a slight downward angle to unify the flowers and container.

5

Turn the container so that two of the horizontal daisy mums plus the top daisy mum form a triangle in front of you. Position a daisy mum in the center of the triangle, making sure it is long enough to create a rounded profile when viewed from the side.

6

Repeat Step 5 for the other two daisy mum triangles.

Add three daisy mums at the edge of the container, one between each of the three already in place at the container edge. Insert the stems to a similar depth as the existing horizontal daisies so that the six daisy mums together give the impression of spokes on a wheel and provide a round outline when viewed from above.

Add more daisy mums around the top daisy, at heights slightly lower than the center flower.

Add more daisy mums to the central area of the design to provide an even distribution of these flowers. Be sure to maintain a rounded profile. A few daisy mums can be cut short and positioned beneath the others, directly against the foam, to provide added depth to the arrangement.

Position spray carnation blossoms and/or buds between the daisy mums at the edge of the container. Allow these flowers to extend to a length ¼" to ½" longer than the daisy mums.

Add enough spray carnations throughout the center of the design to provide even distribution without crowding. Be sure to extend these flowers as far as the spray carnations placed at the edge.

Follow a process similar to the spray carnation placements to add the statice to the design. Use this flower to fill gaps and even out the design form.

VARIATIONS

I. Compact Dinner Table Centerpiece

A single flower type (monobotanical) or single color scheme (monochromatic) provides a nice finished product in this style. Begin by placing the center flower at a maximum height of 14 inches. This will prevent the flowers from blocking the view across the table. Follow the design process described on Pages 24-25, but use more flowers with closer spacing. Be sure to vary the depth of the flowers slightly (Figure 2-5).

II. Meadowlike Round Centerpiece

This variation presents the round centerpiece in a loose and airy form. A mixture of dainty flowers and filler florals, such as *Freesias*, *Delphiniums*, *Lisianthuses*, *Limoniums*, waxflowers, heath asters (*Aster* 'Monte Cassino') and plumosa fern, are good choices due to their light, meadowlike appearances. Follow the same design process, but allow the flowers more freedom to extend beyond the confines of a geometric mound (Figure 2-6).

III. Biedermeier

The Biedermeier design presents the round centerpiece as a tightly spaced, evenly patterned arrangement with concentric rings of color and flower types. To begin, follow Steps 1-3 on Page 24, making sure to select a feature flower, such as a rose, for the top, center placement. Next, finish creating the base ring out of a single flower type. Continue adding rings of flowers, filler flowers and/or foliage until reaching the top flower. Make sure the materials within each ring are placed close together, and keep each ring level as you work around the container (Figure 2-7).

Figure 2-5. Monobotanical compact dinner table centerpiece.

Figure 2-6. Meadowlike round centerpiece.

Figure 2-7. Biedermeier centerpiece.

OBLONG CENTERPIECE

The oblong centerpiece is a horizontal design appropriate for use on a dining table, coffee table or other location in which a long, low floral arrangement is desired. Typically a symmetrical design, the oblong centerpiece is loosely based on a low pyramidal shape (a horizontal isosceles triangle) with the points and edges softened. Frequently, candles are added to provide a soft glow to the flowers.

SUGGESTED MATERIALS

4 lily blooms

8-10 roses

8-10 stems garden *Phlox*

6-8 stems larkspurs

2-3 branched stems spiral *Eucalyptus*

10 stems sword fern

3-4 stems leatherleaf fern

Low, rectangular or oblong dish

Floral foam/mechanics

2-3 taper candles (optional)

2-3 candle adapters (optional)

DESIGN STEPS

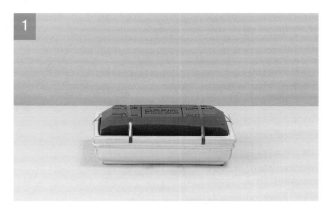

Prepare the container with floral foam.
(See Chapter I, Pages 7-9.)

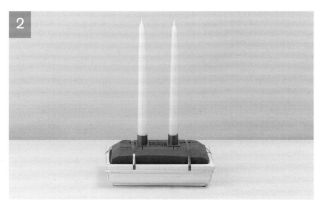

Add candles to the center of the container, if desired.
(See Chapter I, Page 15.)

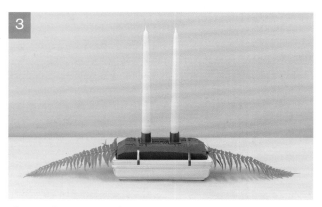

Place a long stem of sword fern into each end of the design dish. Angle the stems downward so they flow onto the table surface.

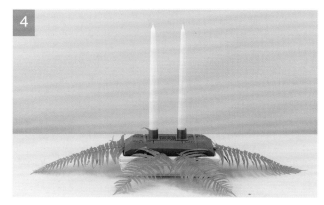

Insert two shorter pieces of sword fern on both long sides of the dish to form a "V"-shape at the edge. The six stems of sword fern should create a skeletal oval outline when viewed from above.

Position the remaining four stems of sword fern so they radiate from the top of the foam outward, with lengths slightly shorter than the previous insertions. If using candles, make sure these stems (and all stems to follow) are no more than ⅓ the height of the candles. This ensures the candles will burn safely.

Use linear stems or side shoots of *Eucalyptus* to fill out the oblong shape. Be sure to extend *Eucalyptus* from the sides as well as the top of the foam, being careful to maintain the established outline.

Cover any visible mechanics and enhance the foliage mix with leatherleaf fern.

Arrange the larkspurs following the same process used for the sword fern (Steps 3-5). Larkspurs with especially long spikes can be cut into segments. Buds from the larkspurs also can be added for texture and interest.

Place two lilies on each side of the centerpiece in staggered positions and with varied flower facings to create a central area of emphasis.

Place two roses at each end to fill out the horizontal line, and place four roses around the candles to fill in the top of the design.

Fill in remaining open areas with garden *Phlox*, making sure to distribute the flowers evenly.

VARIATIONS

I. Diamond Centerpiece

The diamond variation is a more geometric-looking variation of the oblong centerpiece. It derives its form from the one-sided triangle (Pages 19-21), but as a centerpiece, it is two-sided, or all-around. The shape can be somewhat upright or pyramidal, but it is more often long and low so as not to obstruct conversation at the table. To create the diamond centerpiece, follow the same procedure as that of the oblong centerpiece (Pages 28-29), replacing the curved line connections between the tips and sides with straight lines. Instead of the "V" placements in Step 4, place a single piece of foliage in the front and back sides of the foam, perpendicular to the end pieces. The top center also needs clear definition so the centerpiece rises to a point rather than having a rounded top. Strong radiation of larkspurs or other linear flowers from the center out to the edges of the design will help establish the desired diamond shape. Arrange the remaining flowers following the same process as the oblong centerpiece, with an emphasis on straight lines (Figure 2-8).

II. Asymmetrical Horizontal Design

Although most centerpieces are designed symmetrically, they also can be made asymmetrical, providing added style and interest. To do so, begin with outermost horizontal points that are of two different lengths. Strive for a proportional relationship that provides one outermost point that extends one-third the total centerpiece length and the other point that extends two-thirds the total centerpiece length.

This style is especially effective when different flower types are grouped at the ends of the arrangement. Bold flowers in the center provide an important anchor to unify the contrasting ends of the design. This asymmetrical variation might be composed with a long horizontal group of larkspurs and *Eucalyptuses* at one end with a short line of tulips and heath asters at the other. Heather and *Liatrises* positioned at the off-centered point of radiation reinforce the focal area of the tulips and the elongated silhouette of this design (Figure 2-9).

III. Elongated Vegetative Centerpiece

Most centerpieces have a single point of radiation, but the vegetative style offers the opportunity for multiple points of radiation. In this centerpiece variation, arrange the flowers in groups that mimic the natural growth patterns of plants. An elongated container is needed to provide room for three to five or more "plant" groups. Position flowers at varied, natural-looking heights that resist symmetry. Utilize the full depth of the container so that the flower groups are not all lined up on the same plane but, instead, have a realistic haphazardness to their points of emergence out of the "ground" (Figure 2-10).

Figure 2-8. Diamond centerpiece.

Figure 2-9. Asymmetrical horizontal design.

Figure 2-10. Elongated vegetative centerpiece.

ONE DOZEN ROSES IN A VASE

As a traditional symbol of love, roses are frequently sold in dozens. For customers who request the flowers arranged, a vase design, including filler flowers, foliage and ribbon, is the most popular option. Typically, an all-around style is used. For fewer than a dozen flowers, a one-sided style might make a better alternative.

SUGGESTED MATERIALS

12 roses

9 stems leatherleaf fern

6-9 stems tree fern

3 stems baby's breath

Glass vase

3 yards #9-width ribbon

1 wired wood pick

Stem wrap

Waterproof tape

DESIGN STEPS

1

Prepare the container with floral foam, powdered floral foam, shredded plastic foam or marbles (see Chapter I, Page 10), or simply fill the vase with properly prepared flower-food solution. Create a grid with waterproof tape, if desired.

2

Place three stems of leatherleaf fern into the vase, spaced equally apart, so they lie horizontally against the edge of the container and the stems interlock.

3

Position the next three stems of leatherleaf fern, angled slightly more upright, in the spaces between the first trio of stems.

4

Add the remaining three stems of leatherleaf fern to the center of the vase so they stand upright and face each other.

5

Add the tree fern following the same general pattern as the leatherleaf fern. The stems of the greens should be well interlocked and able to support the stems of the roses. If no foam or marbles are used and the greens are not yet supportive, add more foliage before proceeding.

6

Place three roses 3" - 4" apart from one another into the center of the vase so that the stems extend above the vessel at approximately 1½ times the height of the container. The three flowers should form a triangle.

Cut five roses slightly shorter than the first three, and position them equidistant from one another around the container edge so they angle outward. The outline of the design from the top to the edge should appear to form a rounded dome.

Cut the remaining four roses to approximately the same length, and position them between the top flowers and the edge flowers.

Add the three stems of baby's breath, keeping their branched inflorescences intact. Fluff the filler so that it fills out the complete domed shape of the design.

Create a bow (see "Making Bows," Pages 44-46), attach it to a wired wood pick, tape the pick with stem wrap and insert the pick near the edge of the vase.

VARIATIONS

I. One-Sided Half Dozen

When designing a vase arrangement with a limited number of flowers, a one-sided style can provide the greatest impact. For a half-dozen roses, begin with a slightly smaller vase, and place the first stems of leatherleaf fern in the back of the container rather than the center. Use about half as much foliage, and face most of the stems forward to establish a front side. Place the first rose toward the back of the container at a height that is one and one-half times the height of the vase. Next arrange two roses of similar lengths a step down from, and to either side of, the center rose. Then arrange the three remaining roses to form a staggered line above the lip of the container. Place a No. 3-width or No. 5-width ribbon bow at the container edge to provide a well-proportioned finish (Figure 2-11).

II. Rose Bud Vases

A bud vase is the simplest form of vase arrangement, yet it requires careful craftsmanship in order to achieve maximum impact with minimal materials. Two stems of leatherleaf fern provide an adequate foundation in most bud vases. Place these greens so that the stems reach the bottom of the vase and the lowest fern fronds are tucked slightly inside the neck of the vase for stability. Stagger the heights of the fern stems so that one is a step shorter than the other. When both stems of fern are positioned at a height shorter than the planned height of the rose, the flower will be more dominant than if standing in front of a foliage screen. Position the rose at the front and center at a height that is one to one and one-half times that of the vase. If filler flowers are desired, arrange them beneath the rose, and insert a No. 3-width or smaller bow at the container edge (Figure 2-12).

When additional flowers are desired, arrange them so they form a staggered line (Figure 2-13).

Figure 2-11. One-sided half-dozen roses.

Figure 2-12. Single-rose bud vase.

Figure 2-13. Multiple-rose bud vase.

Figure 2-14. Mixed garden flower vase.

Figure 2-15. Mixed garden flower vase.

III. Mixed Garden Flower Vase

A mixed flower combination is a popular alternative to a vase arrangement of a dozen roses. Although the design process is virtually the same, the success of the mixed flower vase relies heavily on combining an interesting blend of flower colors, forms and textures. Garden-inspired combinations are usually very effective and allow seasonal variations. To create a mixed garden vase, follow the steps for a dozen roses in a vase on Pages 32-33, using a combination of three to six types of flowers and filler flowers. Once the first 12 flower placements are made, continue adding floral materials in between while maintaining the generally rounded outline of the bouquet (Figures 2-14, 2-15, 2-16).

Suggested flower mix for spring: *Irises* or tulips, peonies or lilacs, *Freesias* or *Alstroemerias*, *Gerberas* or lilies, heather or *Leptospermum*, and pussy willows or cherry blossoms.

Suggested flower mix for summer: *Delphiniums* or snapdragons; larkspurs or *Liatrises*; *Dahlias* or *Phlox*; daisies, daisy spray mums or cornflowers; and waxflowers or heath asters (*Aster* 'Monte Cassino').

Suggested flower mix for fall: sunflowers or China asters (*Callistephus*), cushion spray mums or carnations, fresh wheat or yarrow, goldenrod (*Solidago*) or statice, and cattails.

Figure 2-16. Mixed garden flower vase.

III

FLOWERS TO WEAR

Flowers worn on the shoulder or on the wrist, in the hair or in a buttonhole have been customary special-occasion attire for decades. The creation of flowers to wear involves a delicate design process. Petite blossoms must be prepared on carefully taped wires. Foliages and fillers must be assembled around the blooms to provide harmonious shapes, colors and textures. Mechanics must be secure yet lightweight. Ribbon and accessories must be controlled so as not to overwhelm the blooms. For their relatively small size, designs of this kind require an inordinate amount of time and skill.

PERSONAL FLOWERS

To master the art of body flowers, a designer must have an understanding of a broad range of mechanical techniques. This chapter provides the fundamentals for preparing and designing flowers into standard styles of flowers to wear. With practice, the gifts of nature's bounty provide the opportunity to create an infinite array of personal flowers for celebrations.

WIRING AND TAPING

The wiring and taping process is a standard means of preparing flowers and foliages for use in flowers to wear. The procedures for completing each of these two stages of flower preparation require considerable practice. Be patient during the learning process, and in time, these skills will become second nature.

Wiring Techniques

Floral wires, ranging in weight from 16 gauge (heavy) to 30 gauge (light) are used to help extend or replace flower stems and control flower placements in designs. As much as possible, the lightest wire that will support the flower or foliage should be used in order to minimize the weight of the finished product. For most corsage and boutonniere work, 24-gauge to 28-gauge wire is ideal. To reduce weight and bulk, trim flower stems to about an inch in length before wiring.

Pierce Wiring

Use the pierce wiring technique for flowers with swollen ovaries (e.g., roses), puffy calyces (e.g., carnations), or thick stems (e.g., *Gardenias*).

Holding a wire close to its end, insert one end into the stem, just beneath the base of the flower, with the wire perpendicular to the stem.

Push the wire through the stem and out the other side until the wire is centered inside the stem. Bend both ends of the wire downward along the stem.

When additional support is needed, cross-pierce the bloom with a second wire in the same manner.

Hook Wiring

Use the hook wiring method for daisy-type flowers, such as spray chrysanthemums.

Insert the wire into the end of the flower stem, and push the wire upward through the bloom's center.

Bend the top of the wire to form a sharp hook about ½" - ¾" long.

Pull the wire downward so the hook is pulled into the center of the flower. The tip of the hook should emerge through the base of the flower. Catch the tip of the hook as the stem is taped to prevent the hook from sliding up and becoming visible in the flower center.

Insertion Wiring

Use the insertion wiring method for flowers that have a single bloom or tight composite bloom on a sturdy stem (e.g., *Dahlias*, peonies, or cushion or button spray mums)

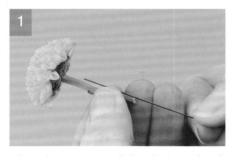

Align the wire parallel with the side of the flower stem.

Slide the end of the wire into the base of the flower until it feels firmly in place. Do not let the wire emerge through the top of the flower. Tape the wire to the stem. Be sure to tape tightly, especially at the stem end.

Wraparound Wiring

Use the wraparound wiring method for clusters of small flowers or fillers that are grouped together into a single unit (e.g., baby's breath, waxflowers or ming fern).

Hold the cluster of flowers together with one hand. Align a wire along the stems, parallel to them, so that the center of the wire is at the base of the blooms.

Wrap the top half of the wire around the stems and the other half of the wire to secure the bundle. Bend the wrapping wire parallel to the stems.

Hairpin Wiring

Use the hairpin wiring method for fragile flowers and foliages (e.g., *Delphinium* florets, stock florets or leatherleaf fern) that cannot be wired using one of the other methods.

Bend a wire to form a hairpin shape.

For flowers, thread both ends of the wire through the top of the blossom, and pull the wire ends down along the stem until the bend in the wire is deep inside the bloom. Wrap one wire around the stem and the other wire.

For foliage, bridge the curved bend of the wire over the midrib of the foliage, and align the two wire ends parallel to the stem. Wrap one wire around the stem and the other wire.

Stitch Wiring

Use the stitch wiring method for broadleaf foliages (e.g., ivy, *Pittosporum* or salal leaves).

Holding a wire perpendicular to a leaf, insert the tip of the wire through the back side of the leaf on one side of the midrib and back through on the other side of the midrib to form a small stitch. This stitch can be made high or low on the leaf depending on the amount of control desired.

Bend the ends of the wire parallel to the stem.

Wrap one wire around the stem and the other wire.

Wiring Techniques for Special Flowers

The "Wiring Chart" on Pages 42-43 provides the recommended wiring techniques for selected flowers and foliages suitable for flowers to wear. The flowers that follow are special types that require their own unique methods.

Stephanotises

Stephanotises can be wired using a variety of techniques depending on the supplies on hand and the look desired.

Stephanotis Stems

Remove the stem and green sepals from beneath the flower, creating a small hole in the base of the flower.

Dip the cotton wick of a commercial *Stephanotis* stem into water; then insert it into the hole at the base of the flower. Push the stem into the flower until the wick is fully inserted.

Hairpin with Accessory

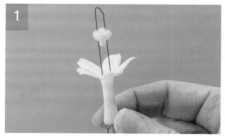

Thread a small piece of moistened cotton onto a hairpin-shaped wire. Using the hairpin method, pull the wire through the flower until it and the cotton rest deep within the throat.

Insert a pearl-headed or gem corsage pin into the center of the flower. The point of the pin will protrude through the base of the stem and should be taped to the flower's stem.

Gardenias

Gardenias are fragile, short-lived blooms with petals that need support. Often, *Gardenias* are sold with ready-made foliage backings attached. In the absence of such a backing, staple four to six small leaves (ivy, salal, *Camellia* or *Gardenia* leaves) to a small cardboard circle, then insert the wired *Gardenia* stem through a hole in the center of the cardboard and slide the backing into place (see Step 2, below).

Cross-pierce the *Gardenia* stem below the blossom with two wires.

Add a small piece of moistened cotton to the end of the stem, and bend the wires parallel to the stem to cage the cotton into position.

Dendrobium Orchids

Dendrobium orchids can be wired in multiple ways depending on the intended use. For most corsage work, the hairpin method is suitable. As an alternative, try the method described here.

Pierce a lightweight wire (26-gauge or 28-gauge) into the thick chin behind the lip of the orchid.

Bend both ends of the wire downward, and align the orchid stem with the wire. Wrap one wire around the stem and the other wire.

Cymbidium, Cattleya and Japhette Orchids

Cymbidium, Cattleya and *Japhette* orchids all can be wired using the same technique. An additional support for the large petals of *Cattleyas* and *Japhettes* is included as a final optional step.

Cross-pierce the stem beneath the flower with two wires.

Add a piece of moistened cotton to the end of the stem, and bend the wires downward, parallel to the stem. The wires will help cage the cotton into position.

For *Cymbidiums* only, carefully reflex the top sepal so it arches backward rather than forward. This will open up the flower face and make it showier.

For *Cattleyas* and *Japhettes*, tape two 22-gauge wires in a color that blends with the petal color. Shape each wire into a narrow loop, and tape the pair of loops to the flower stem. Position the loops so they support the two largest petals on the orchid, and tape the loops into place.

Phalaenopsis and *Vanda* orchids are especially fragile flowers. The shape of these blooms warrants the use of a wiring technique unlike other orchids.

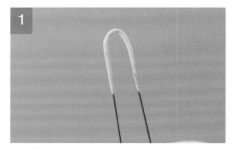

Tape the center of a 26-gauge wire in a color that blends with the flower. Bend the wire into a hairpin shape.

Working from the front side of the bloom, slide the ends of the taped wire into the center of the bloom, being careful to position them so they slide through the natural openings around the throat. The wire should not pierce the flower.

Pull the wire through the middle of the flower until the arched center of the hairpin wire rests at the point where the lip of the orchid meets the protruding column.

From the back of the orchid, insert a 24-gauge wire into the thick central column above the lip of the flower.

Align the three wires parallel with the flower stem. Wrap one end of the hairpin wire around the stem and the other wires.

Wiring Chart

The wiring chart that follows provides a convenient list of selected flowers and foliages suitable for flowers to wear. The recommended wire gauges and wiring techniques may be adjusted to suit each design situation. For flowers to wear, it is always best to use the lightest wire that will support the fresh material.

FOLIAGE	GAUGE	TECHNIQUE	FOLIAGE	GAUGE	TECHNIQUE
Boxwood	24	Wraparound	Ming Fern (cluster)	26	Wraparound
Camellia	24	Stitch	Myrtle (tip)	24	Wraparound
Eucalyptus - seeded (seed cluster)	26	Wraparound	Oregonia	26	Wraparound
			Pittosporum (cluster)	26	Hairpin
Eucalyptus - seeded (leaf)	26	Stitch	*Pittosporum* (leaf)	24	Stitch
Eucalyptus - silver dollar	26	Stitch	Plumosa Fern	28	Wraparound
Eucalyptus - spiral (tip)	26	Wraparound	*Ruscus* - Israeli	26	Stitch
Foxtail Fern (tip)	26	Wraparound	*Ruscus* - Italian (cluster)	26	Wraparound
Geranium	26	Stitch	*Ruscus* - Italian (leaf)	28	Stitch
Ivy	26	Stitch	Salal	26	Stitch
Leatherleaf Fern	26	Hairpin	Sprengeri Fern (cluster)	26	Wraparound

FLOWER	GAUGE	TECHNIQUE	FLOWER	GAUGE	TECHNIQUE
Acacia (cluster)	26	Wraparound	Lily	24	Pierce
Agapanthus (single bloom)	28	Pierce	Lily-of-the-Valley	28	Wraparound
Ageratum	26	Wraparound	*Limonium*	28	Wraparound
Allium, drumstick	24	Insertion	*Lisianthus*	24	Pierce
Alstroemeria (single bloom)	28	Pierce	Monkshood (single bloom)	26	Insertion
Amaranthus	24	Wraparound	Montbretia	24	Wraparound
Aster	24	Insertion	'Monte Cassino' *Aster* (cluster)	26	Wraparound
Astilbe	26	Wraparound	*Narcissus*	24	Insertion
Baby's Breath (cluster)	28	Wraparound	*Nerine* (single bloom)	26	Pierce
Boronia (cluster)	26	Wraparound	*Nigella* - flower	26	Hairpin
Bouvardia	26	Hairpin	*Nigella* - pod	26	Insertion
Bupleurum	26	Wraparound	Orchid - *Cattleya*	24	Cross Pierce*
Calla - miniature	24	Pierce	Orchid - *Cymbidium*	24	Cross Pierce*
Calycina (Thryptomene)	26	Wraparound	Orchid - *Dendrobium*	26	Hairpin or Pierce*
Carnation - miniature	24	Pierce	Orchid - *Japhette*	24	Cross Pierce*
Carnation - standard	22	Pierce	Orchid - *Oncidium* (segment)	28	Hairpin
Celosia	24	Wraparound	Orchid - *Phalaenopsis*	26	Hairpin*
Chrysanthemum - button	24	Insertion	Orchid - *Vanda*	26	Hairpin*
Chrysanthemum - cushion	24	Insertion	Peony	22	Insertion
Chrysanthemum - daisy	22	Hook	Pepperberry (cluster)	24	Wraparound
Cornflower	24	Insertion	Queen Anne's Lace	26	Hairpin
Craspedia	24	Insertion	*Ranunculus*	24	Insertion
Dahlia	22	Insertion	Rice Flower	26	Wraparound
Delphinium (single bloom)	26	Hairpin	Rose - Standard	22	Pierce
Diosma	24	Wraparound	Rose - Spray	24	Pierce
Freesia	24	Wraparound	Rose - Sweetheart	24	Pierce
Gardenia	24	Cross Pierce*	Safflower	24	Insertion
Genista (cluster)	26	Wraparound	*Saponaria* (cluster)	28	Wraparound
Gerbera - miniature	22	Insertion	*Scabiosa*	26	Pierce
Gladiolus (single bloom)	26	Cross Pierce	*Solidago* (cluster)	26	Wraparound
Gloriosa	24	Insertion	*Solidaster* (cluster)	26	Wraparound
Godetia (single bloom)	26	Pierce	Star-of-Bethlehem (single bloom)	26	Pierce
Heather	26	Wraparound	Statice	26	Wraparound
Hyacinth (single bloom)	28	Pierce	*Stephanotis*	26	Hairpin*
Hydrangea (single bloom)	26	Wraparound	Stock (single bloom)	26	Hairpin
Hypericum	24	Hairpin	Sweet pea	26	Wraparound
Kangaroo Paw	26	Wraparound	Tuberose (single bloom)	26	Pierce
Lady's Mantle (cluster)	26	Wraparound	Tulip	24	Pierce
Lavender	28	Wraparound	*Veronica*	26	Wraparound
Larkspur (single bloom)	26	Hairpin	Waxflower	26	Wraparound
Leptospermum	26	Wraparound	Yarrow	24	Hairpin
Lilac (flower segment)	24	Wraparound	*Zinnia*	22	Insertion

See "Wiring Techniques for Special Flowers," Pages 40-42.

43

Taping Flowers and Foliages

Floral tape (stem wrap) is used to wrap the floral wires added to flowers or foliages. Most often, green tape is used to mimic the natural color of stems. When stretched, floral tape becomes somewhat waxy and sticks easily to itself. This allows wire stems to be wrapped with the tape with relative ease. When used properly, floral tape should be smooth and thin, providing a neat finish that blends into the background behind the design.

Start at the top of the flower, holding the end of the tape perpendicular to the stem. Pull enough tape from the roll to provide a few inches of slack. To control the roll, some designers hold the tape on their pinky and ring fingers. Beginners may prefer to tear a piece of tape from the roll for easier handling. A 12" piece should be adequate.

Rotate the flower with one hand while wrapping the tape around the top of the flower stem with the other, overlapping the tape and covering all wire. Stretch the tape so it sticks to itself as you proceed.

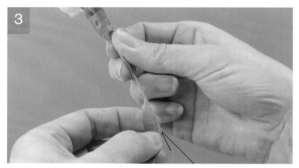

Once the top of the flower stem is wrapped, shift the tape to a downward angle and continue wrapping until the entire wire is covered. Maintain enough tension on the tape so that it stretches consistently throughout the taping process. Too little stretch results in a loose and bulky finish.

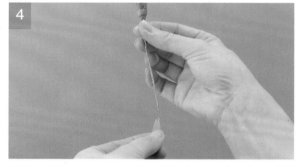

Tear away any excess tape. To thin and tighten the tape, hold the stem at the top and spin it with one hand while sliding the fingers of your other hand down the stem to the base.

MAKING BOWS

There are numerous ways to make bows for corsages and other flowers to wear. Most designers have their preferred methods developed through years of experience. Two techniques, one with a ribbon loop center and one without, are described in this section.

Ribbon sizes for corsages are typically the narrow types including No. ⅛ (sometimes called spaghetti ribbon), No. 1, No. 3 and No. 5. Occasionally No. 9 ribbon is used, as are ribbonlike alternatives such as raffia, bullion wire and decorative wire. The size of a bow should be in proportion to the flowers it will complement. Generally, a small corsage should have a small bow made with narrow ribbon.

Most ribbon has what is considered a front side (shiny) and a back side (dull). Most bows are made with the shiny side out; however, the dull side also can be used for a different texture and appearance. The key is to twist the ribbon before making each loop in order to keep the preferred side of ribbon on the exterior (visible side) of the bow.

Traditional Corsage Bow with Ribbon-Looped Center

When a bow will be featured front and center in a design, it needs a finished center to hide the wire that secures it. This traditional corsage bow is designed with a center loop that hides the wire and provides a finished look. The steps that follow produce a bow featuring the shiny side of the ribbon.

SUGGESTED MATERIALS
2 yards of #3-width ribbon
1 piece of 26-gauge wire
Ribbon shears

DESIGN STEPS

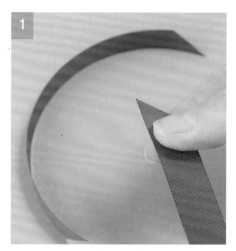

Cut a 5" to 6" length of #3 ribbon, and set it aside. This ribbon will be used to form streamers at the end of the bow-making process. Hold the end of the remaining length of ribbon (66" to 67") between the thumb and index finger, with thumb against the dull side of the ribbon. The rest of the ribbon should hang downward.

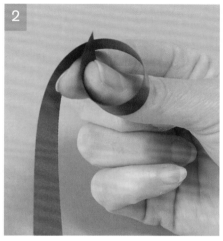

Make a loop with the ribbon loosely over the thumb.

Pinch the two layers of ribbon together between the thumb and index finger. The long end of the ribbon should flow downward as it did at the beginning of the design process.

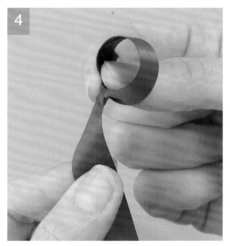

Twist the ribbon so the shiny side faces forward again. Pinch the twist between the thumb and index finger to hold the twisted ribbon in place.

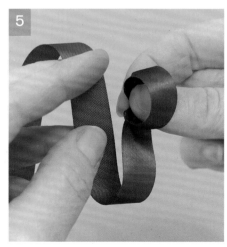

Make a small loop (about 1" long) by flipping the long end of the ribbon back and upward, gathering and pinching the ribbon between the thumb and index finger.

Twist the ribbon again, and pinch the twist between the thumb and index finger to hold it in place. Flip the ribbon back and downward to make another small loop the same size as the first.

7 Make another pair of loops following the same procedure as described in Steps 4-6 on Page 45, but adjust the loop sizes slightly (to about 1½" long).

8 Make another pair of loops slightly larger than the last pair (about 1¾" long).

9 At this stage, if the bow is the desired size, skip to Step 10. If not, make two more pairs of loops both about the same size (for five pairs).

10 Pinch the center of the 5" to 6" length of ribbon cut earlier, and add it to the ribbon gathered between the thumb and index finger.

11 Slide a floral wire through the center loop and under the thumb.

12 Pull the ends of the wire back behind the ribbon, pulling the ribbon loops in the opposite direction.

13 Twist the wire tightly against the ribbon two or three times. A tight twist lends more control to shape the finished bow.

14 Fluff and reposition the loops as needed to create a rounded bow form.

15 Tape the wire before placing in a design.

Simple Tailored Bow

Some corsages call for just a touch of ribbon rather than a full-fledged bow. A tailored look with two simple loops and streamers, much like the common shoe-string bow, is well suited to these designs. Because this type of bow has fewer loops, wider ribbon, such as No. 5 or No. 9, can be used without overwhelming the corsage.

SUGGESTED MATERIALS
12" #5-width or #9-width ribbon
1 piece of 26-gauge wire
Ribbon shears

DESIGN STEPS

Begin by pinching the ribbon between thumb and index finger, with about 2" of ribbon extended away from the pinch.

Form a loop that extends about 1½" from the center, following the same procedure as for a traditional bow.

Create a second loop, leaving the end of the ribbon to form the second streamer. Place a wire into the center of the bow, pull the ends of the wire back behind the bow, and twist the wire tightly against the ribbon two or three times.

Trim the ribbon ends on angles, or create a fishtail finish by cutting an inverted "V" into the end of each streamer. Tape the wire before placing in a design.

Bow Variations

Sometimes a traditional bow does not suit the corsage or other flowers to wear. Variations abound, three of which are provided here.

Wire Bows

Decorative spool wire and bullion wire provide an updated look to modern corsages and other flowers to wear. To make a bow with one of these wires, begin with a short end of wire between the thumb and index finger.

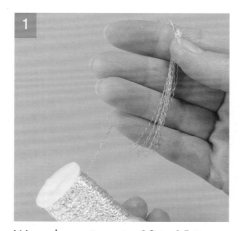

Wrap decorative wire 10 to 15 times around four fingers.

Bind the wire in the center, and fluff the loops into a bowlike form.

Ribbon Loops

For designs where ribbon is desired but there is not a suitable place for a bow, ribbon loops can be used to incorporate tucks of ribbon throughout the design. To make each set of loops, start with an 8-inch to 10-inch piece of ribbon.

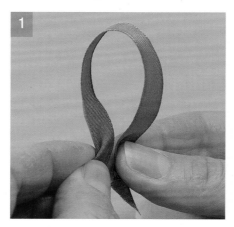

Holding one end of the ribbon, form a loop of the desired size.

Form a second loop, and wire using the wraparound technique (Page 39). Tape the wire before incorporating the loops in a design.

Tulle Poufs

Tulle poufs are a quick and simple way to add softness to corsages and other flowers to wear. Use two squares from a roll of tulle (either the same color or two different colors, depending on the desired effect).

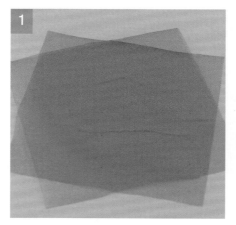

Stack two equal-sized squares of tulle atop each other with corners askew.

Pinch the tulle in the center, and wire this point using the wraparound technique (Page 39). Tape the wire before placing the pouf in a design.

DESIGNING A BOUTONNIERE

Men's boutonnieres are generally small and simple. One or two flowers with an accent of filler and foliage are all that is needed to make a handsome design. Even with these few ingredients, there are almost limitless variations to the look that can be achieved.

Follow the steps below to create a classic single rose boutonniere; then utilize the same general process to create the variations on Page 50.

SUGGESTED MATERIALS

1 rose

3 ivy leaves

3 small sprigs plumosa fern

Wire

Floral tape (stem wrap)

Wire cutters

DESIGN STEPS

Wire and tape all fresh materials. Hold the rose upright, and position a single ivy leaf behind the flower with the base of the leaf at the base of the flower. Tape the leaf stem to the flower stem.

Place the other two leaves at the base of the rose so they extend forward and angle outward, with the three leaves forming a triangular outline. Use the wires stitched through each of the two front ivy leaves to arch them slightly.

Position the sprigs of plumosa fern in the three spaces between the leaves, and tape them into place. Trim the stem to 1½" - 2" long, and tape to cover the boutonniere stem end.

Boutonniere Variations

For tasteful variations on the boutonniere described on Page 49, follow the same steps using any of these flower combinations. Where two feature flowers are used, place the blooms in staggered positions, with the top flower to the left and the bottom flower to the right. For three flowers, stagger the flowers left, right, left.

Two to three *Stephanotises*, *Eucalyptus* and *Genista*

Three *Dendrobium* orchids, Italian *Ruscus* and ming fern

One *Freesia* stem, one lily bud and variegated *Pittosporum* leaves

One or two *Alstroemerias*, *Solidago* and *Ruscus*

Two stock florets, waxflowers and myrtle leaves

A carnation with a wired spray rose threaded through the center

Two miniature carnations and one bud, *Hypericum* and leatherleaf fern

Two spray rose blooms, a *Galax* leaf and ming fern

Simple Corsage

To transform any of the above boutonnieres into a corsage, simply add a small bow at the base of the design (Figure 3-1). Accessories, such as beads or rhinestones, can be added in place of, or in addition to, the filler flowers or foliages (Figure 3-2). A small tulle pouf placed behind the design provides added femininity (Figure 3-3).

Figure 3-1. A bow addition creates a corsage.

Figure 3-2. Jewel accessories added to the filler.

Figure 3-3. A tulle pouf adds femininity.

DESIGNING A CORSAGE

The "single spray" corsage, designed with a tapered shape (narrow at the top and wider at the base) is the classic corsage style. Follow Steps 1-12 to design a classic single spray corsage.

SUGGESTED MATERIALS

5 spray (miniature) carnation buds with color

3 sweetheart or spray roses

2 *Alstroemeria* blossoms

8-10 ivy leaves

5 sprigs statice

1-1½ yards spaghetti ribbon

Floral tape (stem wrap)

Wire

DESIGN STEPS

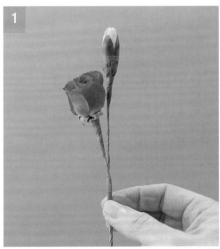

After wiring and taping all materials and making a small corsage bow out of spaghetti ribbon, start with the smallest carnation bud and the smallest rose. Holding the carnation upright, place the rose a step down and to the left. Allow about ½" - 1" of space between the top of the rose and the top of the carnation. Tape the two flower stems together about 2" below the rose. This area of taping will be the binding point of the corsage.

Position another carnation bud to the right of center such that the top of the bud is at the midpoint of the rose head. Tape this flower at the binding point.

Add the next five placements in this sequence—*Alstroemeria*, rose, bow, rose, *Alstroemeria*—following the same left-to-right zigzag pattern. The bow is the exception to this pattern and should be placed in the center. The spacing between the flowers should gradually get closer. The angles of the flowers should shift as well, so that the lower flowers angle forward more than the upper flowers, which stand tall.

Extend a carnation bud on an angle outward and slightly upward beside the lowest rose placement. Counter this placement with a carnation bud extending outward and slightly downward beside the lower *Alstroemeria*. These two carnation buds should form a diagonal line across the corsage. Maintain the same binding point when taping these flowers in place.

Place the final carnation bud on a downward angle to the left side of the base of the corsage so that it falls midway between the previous two carnation buds.

Shape the bow so the loops are carefully incorporated among the flowers.

Create a background of ivy starting at the top of the corsage with the first leaf behind the top carnation bud, then staggering right, left, right and so on to place leaves at the outer edges of the corsage in the spaces between flowers. Only the tips of the leaves should be visible from the front of the corsage.

Finish the foliage background with a pair of leaves that angle downward from under the lowest flowers. These leaves provide a finished quality to the base of the corsage and help cover the mechanics.

Add the sprigs of wired statice throughout the corsage, threading the wires through the flower placements and out the back of the design. Then, bend the wires down to meet the binding point, and tape them into position.

Arch the corsage backward so it will conform to the curve of the shoulder. Adjust the flower placements as necessary to fill any gaps in the design.

Check the corsage from the back to ensure all mechanics are concealed. If needed, add one or two ivy leaves in the back to conceal visible wires.

Trim the corsage stem to a length of 1½" - 2". Wrap the stem with ribbon, if desired.

Glued Filler Variation

Many lightweight flowers and fillers can be glued into corsages and boutonnieres rather than wired and taped. Typically, either floral adhesive or pan-melt glue is used for this purpose. Gluing is efficient but requires a secure base.

In the corsage described above, the statice is light enough to glue into the well-developed network of flowers and greens (Figure 3-4). The *Alstroemerias* are also light enough to be glued in, but in order to do so, the design steps would need to be adjusted so the foliage background is added before the *Alstroemerias* (Figure 3-5). The foliage provides a solid surface behind the flowers for the glue to adhere to.

Figure 3-4. Gluing statice into a corsage.

Figure 3-5. Gluing Alstroemerias *into a corsage.*

Corsage Variations

There are many ways to design a corsage. Some are made with a single large flower, such as a lily or *Cattleya* orchid, accented with tailored foliage and a simple bow (Figure 3-6). Others are a composite of many small flower types that together provide a garden-inspired look (Figure 3-7).

Figure 3-6. Single-bloom corsage.

Figure 3-7. Garden-inspired corsage.

Stem Finish Variations

The standard method of finishing the end of a boutonniere or corsage stem is to tape the wires into a single unit and trim them (with wire cutters) to a length of about 1½ to 2 inches. For a more decorative look, try one of the variations described here.

I. Shapely Stem - Tape the stem as usual (or tape in the manner of the bouquet stem, below), and curve it into a crescent- or "S"-shape (Figure 3-8).

II. Pigtail Stem - Tape the stem as usual, then wrap the stem around a pencil. Slide the pencil out of the wrap to leave a corkscrew tail (Figure 3-9).

III. Bouquet Stem - Tape the wired elements together just beneath the flowers, but do not tape farther down the stem. Flare the individual taped wires apart, and trim them to varied lengths (Figure 3-10).

IV. Ribbon-Wrapped Stem - Tape the stem, and trim it as usual. Then, wrap the stem in ribbon. Start near the end of the stem. Place a dot of hot glue on the stem, and attach the end of a narrow (No. 1 or No. 3) ribbon. Wrap the ribbon downward beyond the end of the stem to form a small tube. Bend the tube up over the stem end and continue wrapping the ribbon up the stem, catching the tube in the ribbon wrap as you go. At the top of the stem, loop the ribbon loosely around the stem, and pull the ribbon end through the loop to make a knot Add a dot of glue, if needed, to secure the knot (Figure 3-11). (Also see Chapter V, Page 110, Steps 2-6.)

V. Decorative Wire Stem - Tape the stem, and trim it as usual. Using a spool of decorative wire or bullion wire, wrap the wire tightly around the stem, starting at the top of the stem and winding downward, overlapping enough to completely conceal the tape. Once the entire stem is covered, wrap upward two or three times, and finish by inserting the end of the spool wire into the weave of the wrap (Figure 3-12).

Figure 3-8. Shapely crescent stems.

Figure 3-9. Pigtail stem.

Figure 3-10. Bouquet stem.

Figure 3-11. Ribbon-wrapped stem.

Figure 3-12. Decorative wire stem.

DESIGNING A WRIST CORSAGE (WRISTLET)

Wrist corsages (wristlets) are popular alternatives to shoulder corsages. The design process for making a wristlet is much like that of a shoulder corsage, yet there are considerable differences in the finished shape and the mechanics. A double spray (or double-ended) corsage, which has a broad center and tapers to a tip at each end, is the style best suited for wristlets. As a shoulder corsage, this style often has a linear quality, but as a wristlet, it is more typically oval in shape.

Wrist corsage holders are available in a variety of styles to attach flowers at the wrist. Some have elastic bands, others have plastic straps, and others are made with hook-and-loop closures (Figure 3-13). Regardless of the holder used, the flowers must be securely attached so they will withstand considerable movement.

The steps that follow describe the process for transforming the corsage described on Pages 51-53 into a wristlet with an elastic band.

Figure 3-13. Varieties of wrist corsage holders.

DESIGN STEPS

SUGGESTED MATERIALS

6 spray (miniature) carnation buds
  with color

5 sweetheart or spray roses

3 *Dendrobium* orchids

11-13 *Camellia* leaves

7 sprigs statice

1-1½ yards spaghetti ribbon
  or bullion wire

Floral adhesive

Floral tape (stem wrap)

Wire

Elastic wristlet

Hot glue gun with glue and/or
  5"-10" additional ribbon

Follow Steps 1-5 on Pages 51-52 for designing a corsage, using *Dendrobium* orchids in place of the *Alstroemerias*. Then, extend the lower portion of the corsage with additional flowers attached at the binding point and bent downward. Add one *Dendrobium* orchid and two roses that continue the zigzag line (left then right). Spacing should increase between these flower placements. Then add a carnation bud to form a tip.

Create a background of *Camellia* leaves starting at the top of the design and staggering placement left to right until reaching the lower tip. Check the corsage from the back to ensure all mechanics are concealed. If needed, add one or two *Camellia* leaves in the back to conceal visible wires.

Arch each end of the corsage backward so that it will conform to the curve of the wrist. Adjust the flower placements as necessary to fill any gaps in the design. Add sprigs of statice throughout the design, securing them into the corsage with floral adhesive.

Trim the stems to a length of 1½" - 2". Using wire cutters, cut one wire at a time. After cutting, cover the ends of the exposed wires with floral tape.

Align the stem of the corsage along the metal plate of the wristlet. Fold the flanges that extend from the sides of the metal plate over the stem of the corsage.

For added security, carefully tie one or two pieces of ribbon around the wrist-let plate, over the corsage stem, and into a knot. The ends of the ribbon can remain visible as a design accent, or they can be cut short. If the flowers feel loose on the wristlet, apply a line of hot glue on each side of the stem along the metal plate.

Once the corsage is attached to the wristlet, adjust the flowers so they arch over the sides of the wristlet. The finished design should lie gracefully on the wrist.

Glued Wristlet Variation

To speed the design process and maintain a lightweight finished product, glue lightweight flowers, fillers and foliages into wristlet designs. Start by creating a fluffy bow comprising multiple ribbon types and sizes. Tulle can be used as well, either alone or mixed with ribbon.

Tie a bow to a wristlet with a pair of streamers from the bow.

Glue foliage into the bow to thicken the foundation for the flowers.

Glue flowers into the design. Apply floral adhesive to the floral stems, and insert the stems into the base.

57

Flowers worn in the hair make any outfit and occasion more special. Weddings and proms are two of the most popular occasions for hair flowers. At events such as these, dancing and movement are to be expected, and hair flowers must be comfortable and secure. In addition, different hair types dictate different hair flower mechanics. Several simple hair flower options are provided here.

Pin-on Hair Cluster

A single blossom or cluster of flowers tucked behind the ear or pulled to the side or back of the head is the classic floral hair adornment. For this type of design, light-weight flowers (such as *Stephanotises*, sweet peas, *Delphinium* florets, *Dendrobium* orchids, baby's breath and *Genista*) on lightweight wires are the best choices. Generally, greens and fillers should be kept to a minimum. The floral cluster described here is intended to be attached with bobby pins. Alternative hair attachment methods are described in the variations.

SUGGESTED MATERIALS
2 *Dendrobium* orchids
3 ivy leaves
2-3 small sprigs waxflowers
Floral tape (stem wrap)
Wire, Pencil
Floral adhesive
Bobby pin

DESIGN STEPS

Wire and tape the three ivy leaves, and stack them on top of one another all facing the same direction. Tape the leaves into a single unit, wrapping only a ½" width with the floral tape.

Fan two of the ivy leaves out away from the third, rotating one of the leaves 180 degrees. Curl each of the wired ivy stems around a pencil to create pigtail stems (see Page 54).

Remove the stems from the *Dendrobium* orchids, and apply a small amount of floral adhesive to the back of each bloom. Apply floral adhesive to the ivy leaves as well. Glue the orchids onto the ivy leaves with their throats facing the center and touching each other. Glue two or three small sprigs of waxflowers to the ivy leaves around the orchids. Clip a jeweled bobby pin to the stems for placement in the hair.

Hair Cluster Variations

When bobby pins will not adequately secure a flower cluster, alternative hair accessories are necessary. Here, variations are described for hair clips, combs and headbands.

Hair Combs and Hair Clips

Common hair combs and spring-type hair clips make good bases for simple hair clusters. Unadorned versions of both of these accessories are readily available in craft and fabric stores. When necessary, decorative combs and clips also can be used. To design the pin-on hair cluster as a comb or clip, follow these steps.

Glue a pair of ivy leaves, base to base, across the top of the comb (or clip).

Glue a *Phalaenopsis* orchid, or a small collection of fillers, atop the leaves.

Headbands

A headband provides a secure base for hair flowers. An inexpensive plastic headband can be covered with a row of overlapping leaves or flower petals to dress it up (Figure 3-14). With this foliage base, the flowers can be glued directly to the headband (Figure 3-15). When using a decorative headband, design a wired and taped cluster as described on Page 58. Then securely tie the cluster of flowers to the headband with ribbon.

Figure 3-14. Ivy leaves glued onto a headband.

Figure 3-15. Flowers glued to the ivy-leaf base.

Floral Wreath

The floral wreath is a classic hair accessory. It can be designed completely with flowers (baby's breath is traditional), completely with foliage (ivy is traditional) or with a combination of materials (such as ivy, baby's breath and spray roses). The traditional baby's breath wreath is described here. Because head sizes vary greatly, it is best to take a head measurement of the wearer so the design can be correctly sized.

DESIGN STEPS

SUGGESTED MATERIALS

3-5 stems baby's breath
2½-3 yards narrow ribbon
2 20-gauge wires (18" in length)
1 26-gauge wire
Floral tape (stem wrap)

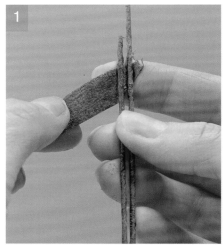

Tape each length of 20-gauge wire with floral tape. Then tape the two wires together, overlapping them about 2" in the center to create one long wire.

Bend one end of the wire into about a 1" hook, and tape half of the hook to form a small loop. Measure the wire, and cut it to match the head measurement of the wearer.

Starting at the looped end of the wire, tape a small cluster of baby's breath to the wire, with the flowers covering the loop.

Position a second cluster of baby's breath so the flowers cover the stems of the first cluster. Tape the cluster into place.

Continue adding clusters of baby's breath in this manner, maintaining a consistent cluster size, until reaching the other end of the wire. Tape the last cluster in place leaving 1" of wire at the end.

Design a small bow with multiple streamers of varied lengths. Wire and tape the stem of the bow, then tape it onto the end of the baby's-breath-covered wire, leaving enough wire to bend into a small hook.

Bend the wire hook through the loop at the other end of the headband, and pinch the hook tightly to secure the ends of the wreath together. Shape the wire into an even circle, and adjust the bow so the streamers flow freely downward.

Wreath Variations

Ivy Wreath - For a classic halo of ivy, follow Steps 1 and 2 for the floral wreath. Then, wrap individual strands of ivy around the wire, taping occasionally as needed to hold the ivy in place. Overlap multiple strands of ivy to achieve the desired fullness. Follow Steps 5-7 to complete the wreath, omitting the ribbon if desired (Figure 3-16).

Figure 3-16. Ivy wreath with ribbon wound through.

Combination Flower and Foliage Wreath - To combine flowers, fillers and foliages in a wreath, create a foliage base using the process described for the ivy wreath above. Then, glue flowers and fillers into place with floral adhesive, or wire the blooms and tape them to the wire frame. Space the accent materials evenly so that the wreath appears balanced when placed in the hair (Figure 3-17).

Figure 3-17. Combination flower and foliage wreath.

IV

SYMPATHY
ARRANGEMENTS

Some of the most important arrangements made by florists are funeral designs. Floral options for funerals include flowers placed on the casket, in the casket and beside the casket. These final tributes from family and friends are typically large floral displays that require special mechanics.

This chapter provides the design fundamentals for each major type of sympathy arrangement. Variations provide examples of alternative design shapes and mechanics. Designers can personalize the floral tributes for any funeral by using these styles and variations, modifying color and flower choices as needed, and adding symbols and mementos representative of the careers, hobbies and interests of the deceased.

TRADITIONAL SYMPATHY BASKET

Basket arrangements are among the most popular sympathy tributes. The shape of most traditional sympathy baskets is either a one-sided triangle (see Chapter II, Page 19) or a fan, where flowers of the same stem length radiate in an arc.

Sympathy baskets are known by a variety of terms. Once designed primarily in papier-mâché containers, these arrangements are still referred to as "mâchés" by some florists. The manner in which the flowers radiate from the center of the design inspires another common term, "spray" (the flowers appear to spray from the center outward).

Regional names abound, including "glad basket," in reference to the common use of *Gladioli* as a primary flower, and "showy basket" or simply "showy," describing the big display desired. Many sympathy "baskets" aren't designed in what most would consider a true basket. In some cases, plastic containers with handles give a basketlike look. In others, the containers have no handle.

The sympathy basket that follows features a traditional flower mix to create a large symmetrical triangular spray. Before designing this arrangement, it may be helpful to review the steps for the one-sided symmetrical triangle described in Chapter II (Pages 19-21).

SUGGESTED MATERIALS
8 *Gladioli*
8 snapdragons
3 cremone chrysanthemums
7 roses
13 carnations
10-12 stems flat fern
3-5 stems leatherleaf fern
2 stems salal
Sympathy basket
Floral foam
Chicken wire
Waterproof tape
20 20-gauge wires

DESIGN STEPS

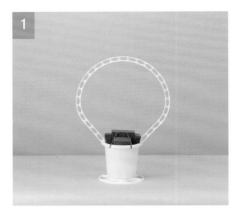

1

Fill the container with floral foam, cover with chicken wire, if desired, and secure with waterproof tape (see Chapter I, Pages 7-9).

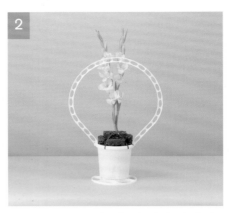

2

Position a pair of tall *Gladioli* of slightly varied heights to establish the top point of the triangle. For maximum impact, the center line formed by these flowers should be twice the height of the container. If using a container with a handle, place the *Gladioli* behind the handle.

3

Place a *Gladiolus* on each side of the center flowers, 3" - 4" shorter than the center flowers. The angle of these two flowers should be about 30 degrees from the vertical line. Extend a *Gladiolus* horizontally on each side of the container. Place a *Gladiolus* in the space that remains on each side of the design, at about 60-degree angles from the vertical line. Vary the lengths of these stems slightly. Be sure the *Gladioli* are inserted securely.

4

Repeat the triangular shape of the design by arranging several stems of flat fern in a radiating pattern in the spaces between and behind the *Gladioli*. Arrange two or three additional stems of flat fern horizontally across the front edge of the container, at a slight downward angle.

5

Fill in the center of the design with the salal, followed by the leatherleaf fern. Be sure all stems appear to radiate from the center outward.

6

Add a few pieces of foliage to the back of the design to cover the floral foam and mechanics.

7

Arrange two snapdragons to extend outward from the front edge of the container to form a broad "V." Place two more snapdragons between the center and side *Gladioli*, also forming a "V." Add two more snapdragons to each side.

8

Place the three cremone mums in the center of the design in a triangular formation to create a focal area. Position the flowers about 2" - 3" apart.

9

Wire the stem of each carnation and rose with a 20-gauge wire. Insert the tip of the wire into the calyx of each carnation and the ovary of each rose, then gently wrap the wire around the stem in a downward spiral.

10

Create a stair-stepped line down the center with five carnations. The flowers should shift from upright facings at the top to forward facings at the bottom.

11

Extend three carnations out each side of the design, filling the most open spaces and spacing these flowers similarly to the other carnations.

12

Place one more carnation between the top of the design and the outermost side carnation on each side of the design. Arrange three roses stairstepped through the center of the design and two more roses on each side.

VARIATIONS

Variations on the symmetrical triangle or fan-shaped sympathy basket arrangement are many. Sometimes the look of the design can be shifted simply by changing the type of container used. Grouping the flowers instead of mixing them also provides a different look. Adjusting the balance from symmetrical to asymmetrical and incorporating an accessory, such as a candle, figurine or framed photo, lends a sense of style and originality. With the wide range of flowers and foliages available, the possibilities are endless. The variations that follow provide examples of the diverse options for this important sympathy design style.

I. "Half and Half" Triangle

This simple symmetrical triangle variation uses grouping to divide the design into two zones, with stocks forming the top half and carnations forming the bottom half. If desired, a bow can be used in the center to connect and unify the zones.

To design this arrangement, start with a tall stock (one and one-half to two times the height of the container) in the center of the foam. Stair-step additional stocks at shorter lengths on each side of the center stock, allowing the spikes to angle slightly away from the center and form a narrow triangle. Add one or two short spikes to the center of this triangle. Place a line foliage, such as myrtle or *Eucalyptus*, in the spaces between the flowers.

Lightly green the base of the design using foliage to extend a horizontal line across the container. Arrange three or four carnations on each side of the center to enhance the horizontal line. Cluster three to five carnations together in the middle of the design just beneath the lowest stocks. Add carnations as needed to connect the side carnations with the center (Figure 4-1).

II. Monobotanical Fan

Sympathy baskets often are designed with mixed materials including line flowers used to establish strong radiation and a clear outline. This variation uses only one flower type (thus the name monobotanical) in a round form versus line form. Mixed foliages, including some linear types, enhance the texture and interest.

Create a fan-shaped outline by arranging several stems of myrtle, all of the same length, into the foam starting at the top center position (vertical placement) and progressing in an arc (diagonal placements) to each side (horizontal placements). Green the rest of the container with additional myrtle as well as huckleberry, salal and/or leatherleaf fern.

Wire 36 to 50 carnations using the technique described in Step 9 on Page 65. Establish an arc of carnations in front of the foliage outline. Then arrange several carnations horizontally along the front edge of the container. Establish a focal point in the center with several carnations grouped and spaced closer than the perimeter flowers. Use the remaining carnations to connect the focal flowers to the perimeter, placing some of the flowers deep within the design and the rest of the flowers on the surface (Figure 4-2).

III. Triangular Spray with Groupings

Sympathy designs termed "sprays" are frequently characterized by strong radiation from the center of the container outward. When the radiating materials are grouped rather than mixed throughout the arrangement, the resulting design has a modern feeling, often with a sense of garden inspiration.

To create a triangular spray with groupings, begin with three clusters of linear materials (such as bells-of-Ireland, heather, heath asters, larkspurs, stocks or *Delphiniums*) placed to form the three points of a triangle. Make each cluster about the same size to maintain a feeling of balance.

Add a cluster of focal flowers (such as lilies, *Gerberas* or roses) to the center. Extend two or three additional focal flowers vertically toward the top point of the triangle. Add two or three more flower, filler or foliage clusters, as needed, to help fill vacant spaces and unify the groupings (Figure 4-3).

Figure 4-1. "Half and Half" triangle.

Figure 4-2. Monobotanical fan.

Figure 4-3. Triangular spray with groupings.

CASKET SPRAY

Sprays often are used to cover the casket during a funeral or memorial service. Full-couch casket sprays are used when the casket will be fully closed throughout the funeral or memorial service and typically are designed to cover most or all of the casket lid. Half-couch casket sprays adorn the foot end of a half-open casket.

Most full-couch sprays are long and low with an oblong or pointed oval outline, which is described here. An alternative style for the half-couch casket spray is an asymmetrical design with the focal point offset to the left and the longer flowers extended to the right, toward the foot of the casket.

SUGGESTED MATERIALS
10 *Gladioli*
3-5 stems lilies
36-48 roses
¾ bunch emerald palm
⅔ bunch leatherleaf fern
½ bunch plumosa fern
Leaf shine, optional
Large pre-assembled
  casket saddle or
Large casket saddle,
  floral foam, chicken wire
  and waterproof tape
36 20-gauge wires

DESIGN STEPS

1 Soak a large pre-assembled casket saddle or large floral-foam-filled cage, or prepare an empty saddle with floral foam, chicken wire and waterproof tape (see Chapter I, Pages 8-9).

2 Trim the tips of each piece of emerald palm with ribbon shears. Remove about 1" - 1½" from each tip following the natural shape of the leaf so the foliage becomes less floppy and more tailored.

3 Arrange a long stem of emerald palm into each end of the saddle. Place a third piece of palm into the front center base of the foam, extending downward. Place a shorter stem of palm extending from the center of the back side of the foam.

4 Visualize a line connecting the center tip to each side tip, and add two or three pieces of emerald palm extending from the edge of the casket saddle along each of these lines. Be sure all of these placements appear to radiate from the center. Use two to four pieces of emerald palm to connect the points across the back edge of the saddle.

5 Fill in the design outline with the remaining pieces of emerald palm, beginning with two or three stems inserted into the top center of the foam. These stems should be about 8" - 10" long and angled so they rise no more than about 6" above the foam. Continue adding stems of palm at different levels until the framework is complete.

6 Fill in the framework and cover most mechanics with leatherleaf fern. (If a glossy look is desired, spray the completed foliage arrangement lightly with leaf shine.)

7 Arrange two long stems of *Gladioli* into each end of the casket saddle. Insert these stems deeply into the foam and angle them downward so they flow onto the table surface.

8 Arrange two shorter *Gladioli* (about half the length of the end flowers) in the center of the front edge of the casket saddle to form a "V." Place two additional *Gladioli* in a "V" pattern at the back edge of the saddle, extending no farther than the foliage. Add a single *Gladiolus* between the center *Gladioli* and those on the ends.

9 Establish the focal area in the center of the design with lilies, either placed in clusters as they grow or removed from the stem and inserted individually. The height of the lilies should establish the peak of the dome-shaped design.

10

Wire the roses using the technique described in Step 9 of the traditional sympathy basket on Page 65. Place several roses in a zigzag line from the center of the design's dome downward through the focal area.

11

Arrange roses to extend to the front edges of the design outline, and place additional roses in a zigzag line from each side tip to the focal area. Place more roses to connect the focal area to the back of the design. When correctly placed into the domed formation, many of the flowers on the back side of the design will not be visible from the front.

12

Fill gaps in the design and unify the various flower types with the remaining roses. Cut some of the roses shorter than others, and place them to create depth, particularly among the lilies.

13

Arrange the plumosa fern throughout the design to unify and soften it. Place the longest plumosa tips among the *Gladioli*. Other stems can be cut into segments and placed through the center of the design.

VARIATIONS

There are many ways to alter the appearance of the traditional full-couch casket spray. Often, a few adjustments in the flower mix result in a different finished appearance. Small changes in flower positioning also can provide notable variations in the finished design shape.

The half-couch casket spray, placed on the foot end of a half-open casket, is frequently designed as a smaller version of a full couch. In fact, many full- and half-couch designs are interchangeable. By using fewer flowers, a full couch can be designed as a half couch; and by using more flowers, a half couch becomes a full couch. The following casket spray variations reflect several design possibilities that can be scaled up or down to suit the needs of the individual casket.

I. Monobotanical Full Couch
Traditional casket sprays are often designed with a mix of flower types and a strong foliage outline. This spray uses one feature flower (roses) and an accent botanical (*Hypericum*) with little foliage. Subtle variations in the rose colors help provide contrast and interest (Figure 4-4).

To design this spray, follow Steps 3-6 on Page 68 to green the casket saddle, replacing the emerald palm with smaller foliages, such as salal or huckleberry. Shorten the lengths of these foliages so they extend only slightly beyond the casket saddle. Establish the design outline as described in Steps 7-9 on Page 68 with roses instead of *Gladioli* and lilies, and then complete the shape with more roses as described in Steps 11-12 on Page 69. Use *Hypericum* in place of plumosa to fill gaps and unify the rose placements.

II. Oval Half Couch with Scarf
The traditional full-couch spray can be reduced in size to create a smaller spray appropriate for making a simple statement on a fully closed casket or for covering the foot end of a half-open casket. A monochromatic approach, as demonstrated here with white *Freesias* and white spray roses, provides strong impact despite the smaller size of the finished composition. A coordinating fabric sash, afghan, tartan or runner draped across the casket enhances the appeal of this tasteful display (Figure 4-5).

Green a half-couch casket saddle with leatherleaf fern, tree fern, plumosa and/or princess pine. Approach the design process like that of an oversized centerpiece (see Chapter II, Pages 27-29), providing slightly more height, but with less extension to points on each end. Follow Steps 7-12 on Pages 68-69 to develop the modified shape in proportion to the smaller base. Concentrate more flowers through the center of the spray; allow open spaces around the flowers near the edges.

Figure 4-4. Monobotanical full couch.

III. Pyramidal Half Couch

The pyramidal half couch is another casket spray variation that uses a centerpiece format to guide flower placements. This design takes cues from the diamond centerpiece (Chapter II, Page 30) in which lines are straight and points are exaggerated. Here, a mixed flower combination is used for a garden-inspired look (Figure 4-6).

Follow Steps 3-4 on Page 68 for the full-couch casket spray, using ti leaves instead of emerald palm to develop a pointed outline. Fill in the center of the casket saddle with short pieces of leatherleaf fern or salal. Establish the outer points and the tip of the design with snapdragons and roses, then angle stems downward at the front edge of the casket saddle to flow across the curve of the casket lid. Extend additional snapdragons through the center of the design, then create a dominant focal area with roses. Fill the gaps between the flower placements with *Delphiniums*, *Freesias*, *Solidago* or other garden blooms.

IV. Accessorized Spray

Following the trend toward greater personalization of sympathy designs, this casket spray uses a framed portrait of the deceased as the focal point in a scaled-down version of the traditional full-couch spray. *Gerberas* placed at the base of the photograph enhance the central focal emphasis (Figure 4-7).

Begin this spray by securing the mechanics needed to stabilize the photo frame. Attach a pair of wood picks or hyacinth stakes to the back of the frame with waterproof tape, or aisle-runner tape, and push them deeply into the foam to secure the frame in the center of the casket saddle.

Follow Steps 3-4 on Page 68 for the full-couch casket spray, using salal instead of emerald palm to develop the outline of the design. Fill in the center with additional foliage, and cover the mechanics on the back of the frame with foliage as well.

Extend bells-of-Ireland, larkspurs, snapdragons and/or stocks in a radiating pattern from the edges of the saddle to the tips of the outline. Develop the focal area at the base of the frame using *Gerberas*, roses and tulips. Make sure none of these flowers rises so high that it obscures the portrait. Enhance the design with roses and tulips, and fill in with *Solidago* and/or *Hypericum* (Figure 4-7).

Figure 4-5. Oval half couch with scarf.

Figure 4-6. Pyramidal half couch.

Figure 4-7. Accessorized spray.

V. Garden Mix with Groupings

A broad mix of flowers results in a design that looks quite different from the traditional casket spray of three to four flower types. When the many flower types are grouped rather than scattered throughout the design, the look is even more dynamic. This variation uses garden flowers segmented into individual wedges around a traditional pointed oval silhouette.

Follow Steps 1-6 on Page 68 for the traditional full couch using assorted foliages such as salal, myrtle, Italian *Ruscus* and/or huckleberry in place of the emerald palm. Imagine the design outline divided into eight pielike wedges. Ribbon can be used to temporarily mark the wedges.

Radiate a different flower type from the center to the edge of each of the eight wedges. Vary the flower forms to create an interesting mix. Allow a few flowers from some groups to mix among the flowers in the wedges beside them. Place two or three focal flowers (such as *Irises*, lilies, *Gerberas*, roses or *Hydrangeas*) in the focal area to add impact and unify the groups. Allow a few of these central flowers to meander into a couple of nearby wedges as well (Figure 4-8).

VI. Tied Bouquet

This design, constructed in a casket saddle, displays the flowers like a presentation bouquet. Natural flower stems radiate to the left, with blossoms extending to the right. The collection is "tied" at the joining point with a ribbon accent.

Create the outline for the design with flat fern, leatherleaf fern, sprengeri fern, plumosa fern and/or Italian *Ruscus*, with the longest stems extending 15 inches or more off the right corner of the saddle. Place shorter stems of foliage around the edges of the saddle to cover the mechanics.

Extend line flowers such as snapdragons, bells-of-Ireland, larkspurs, *Liatrises* and/or stocks toward the right corner of the design outline, varying the stem lengths and broadening the spray near the point of radiation. Add mass and form flowers, such as tulips, lilies, *Lisianthuses*, *Irises* and/or chrysanthemums to the broad base of the bouquet. Anchor the design with a few large flowers such as *Hydrangeas* or football mums at the binding point. Add filler flowers such as *Leptospermums*, waxflowers or *Solidago*.

Save the stem ends cut from the flowers during the design process. Place these stems in a radiating pattern out the back left corner of the casket saddle. Trim the stems as needed to make a neat and even bouquet stem look (Figure 4-9).

Figure 4-8. Garden mix with groupings.

Figure 4-9. Tied bouquet.

EASEL SPRAY

Flowers displayed on easels are prevalent at funerals in many parts of the United States. Traditional easel sprays, also referred to as standing sprays, are typically mass designs with flowers radiating from the center outward to form a diamond or oval shape. Easel sprays are generally presented facing forward on wood or wire easels. The focal point can be positioned in the center or upper half of the spray. Mechanics for these designs vary, including a variety of floral-foam bases into which flowers are arranged directly as well as plastic foam, such as Styrofoam® brand plastic foam, into which flowers are arranged in water tubes, secured to wood picks or clamped with metal picks. In this example, a floral-foam cage is used.

SUGGESTED MATERIALS

10 snapdragons

30-35 roses

8 carnations

10 stems emerald palm

½ bunch leatherleaf fern

½ bunch seeded *Eucalyptus*

Floral-foam cage

Wire easel

2 green chenille stems

30 20-gauge wires

3-4 yards of #40-width ribbon

4″ wired wood picks

DESIGN STEPS

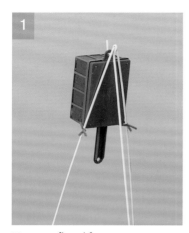

1 Hang a floral-foam cage on a wire easel. Secure the cage to the legs with green chenille stems (or taped 22-gauge wires).

2 Trim 1" - 1½" from the tips of each piece of emerald palm, following the natural shape of the leaf so the foliage becomes more tailored.

3 Insert two roughly equal emerald palm stems into the floral-foam cage to form a vertical line. Angle these stems to follow the slant of the easel.

4 Cut four stems of emerald palm to a length about ⅔ that of the first placements. Arrange these stems to form "V" shapes on each side of the foam cage.

5 Place one stem of emerald palm in each of the four spaces between the vertical palms and the side palms.

6 Green the center of the design with leatherleaf fern so that it radiates from the center of the foam to the base of the emerald palm.

7 Follow the outline created with the palm leaves to place 10 snapdragons around the edge of the foam.

8 Wire each rose stem with 20-gauge wire (see Step 9, Page 65). Place the first three roses in a zigzag pattern in the center of the design, extending forward about 4" - 6".

9 Extend the zigzag line from top to bottom with six more roses. Next, arrange two roses horizontally on each side of the design.

Arrange two roses in each of the four spaces between the top and bottom points and the side points. Place another seven roses to add depth to the center.

Arrange eight carnations to connect the placements, even out the spacing and fill any significant gaps, leaving a moderate opening in the center.

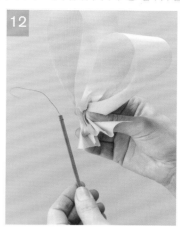

Make single and double ribbon loops, 4" - 5" long, with #40-width ribbon. Wire each loop or pair of loops with a wired wood pick. Wire several lengths of ribbon to individual wood picks for use as streamers.

Place the picked loops and streamers into the center of the spray to provide a bowlike appearance. Weave the streamers among the flowers. Add one to five roses into the center at a height above the ribbon.

Arrange stems of seeded *Eucalyptus* throughout the design to soften and unify all parts of the design.

VARIATIONS

There are many ways to vary the look of an easel spray. Instead of a mix of flower forms, a design of all mass flowers or all line flowers looks notably different from the traditional example described previously. Changing the shape from an oval to a diamond, triangle, circle or crescent adds variety as well. Shifting the position of the spray on the easel provides yet another opportunity to make the design distinctive. Several of these design concepts are represented in the variations that follow.

I. Tropical Spray

A strong tropical look can be achieved with the use of bold foliages and a single exotic flower type, such as the *Cymbidium* orchid sprays used here (Figure 4-10).

Follow Steps 3-4 on Page 74 using large tropical foliages (such as *Monstera*) for the vertical placements and narrow tropical leaves (such as variegated *Aspidistra*) for the horizontal placements. Supplement the initial foliage placements with additional leaves that radiate naturally from the center outward.

Create a strong vertical line through the center of the design with orchids or another showy tropical flower that is well proportioned to the foliage (such as *Anthuriums*, birds-of-paradise or *Heliconias*). Counter the vertical line with a few additional flowers that radiate horizontally across the center of the design.

II. Tied Bouquet Spray

The tied bouquet, as an easel design, is similar to the casket spray of the same name illustrated on Page 72. Attach a floral-foam cage to an easel, and arrange lilies in a loosely radiating manner to mimic the appearance of a bouquet of flowers gathered from the garden. Position the flowers closer together at the base of the foam, allowing more open space at the perimeter.

Add a ribbon bow beneath the focal flowers. Then add bare flower stems to the base of the foam so they radiate widely, providing a natural gathered appearance. Trim the ends of the stems neatly (Figure 4-11).

III. Cascading Spray

This variation combines an obtuse-angle scalene triangle (Chapter II, Page 22) with the dramatic flow of a cascade bouquet (Chapter V, Pages 91-93) for a creative twist on the traditional easel design.

Attach a retangular floral-foam cage vertically to an easel. Establish the three main points of the design with Italian *Ruscus*, with the longest stem extending from the base of the cage toward the right. Position the shortest stems of *Ruscus* horizontally to the left, and extend a midlength stem of *Ruscus* vertically with a slant to the right.

Add branches and bark to the foliage base to create rustic charm, then create a strong focal point and enhance the design silhouette with roses (Figure 4-12).

Figure 4-10. Tropical spray.

Figure 4-11. Tied bouquet spray.

Figure 4-12. Cascading spray.

76

SYMPATHY WREATH

Wreaths, symbolic of the circle of life, are appropriate designs for funeral and memorial services. Typically displayed on easels, wreaths can be designed on many types of circular bases. Grapevine or other natural wreaths accented with floral clusters are common, as are floral-foam wreath rings completely covered in flowers. Plastic-foam wreaths wrapped in ribbon or covered with fresh leaves are sometimes used as well.

In comparison to many other sympathy designs, wreaths are one of the few styles that are suited to smaller and shorter-stemmed flower types. Here, a flower-covered wreath is designed using a broad mix of flowers and foliages.

SUGGESTED MATERIALS

4-6 *Hydrangeas*
12-15 roses
8-10 miniature callas
5-7 stems garden *Phlox*
10-15 *Freesias*
55-60 *Galax* leaves
Floral-foam wreath
Wire easel
22-gauge wire
Waterproof tape

DESIGN STEPS

1 Soak a floral-foam wreath form, then wrap ¼" waterproof tape around it several times to reinforce the form.

2 Hang the wreath on the hook of a wire easel. Bind the form onto the easel by wrapping taped wires around the wreath and both front easel legs. For wreaths with a papier-mâché base, an alternative attachment method involves inserting a Dixon® pin or a greening pin over each front easel leg, from behind, and into the back of the mâché-backed wreath form.

3 Arrange *Galax* leaves around the interior and exterior edges of the wreath form. If desired, collapse the legs of the easel so the wreath can be placed flat onto a counter or table for designing.

4 Arrange short-stemmed roses individually and in groups of twos and threes, with the base of each rose resting atop the surface of the foam. Vary the flower facings so that some roses face forward and others face upward, downward and to the sides.

5 Arrange the *Hydrangeas* and *Phlox* throughout the wreath to fill in and cover the remaining mechanics.

6 Arrange the miniature callas among the roses and around the edges of the wreath frame. Tuck in the *Freesias,* to fill in the gaps and unify all of the elements.

VARIATIONS

Wreaths are sometimes designed in oval, rectangular and even square shapes, and may feature framed photos, personal mementos or symbolic accessories in the center. Each of these variations is distinctive in its own way.

I. Patterned Placements

This oval wreath features floral materials arranged in a striped pattern, with each element grouped tightly and repeated several times. In this type of design, foliages can be placed as separators between stripes.

Prepare the mechanics following Steps 1 and 2 on Page 78. Create a pattern around the interior circle of the wreath to set the plan for the stripes.

Begin creating dense flower stripes, with the flower stems cut short and the blooms placed close together and close to the foam. Place the smaller blooms in each stripe at the inner edge of the wreath and the largest flowers at the outer edge. Additional short stripes may need to be added toward the outer edge to fill in the oval or circular wreath shape (Figure 4-13).

Figure 4-13. Wreath with patterned flower placements.

II. Contemporary Square

Square-shaped floral-foam forms have a modern look that is well suited to contemporary designs. Though some contemporary arrangements require advanced skills, others can be accomplished with only small deviations from traditional techniques.

Here, the square wreath form is covered in patterned flower placements much like the oval wreath above. A contemporary look is added by intersecting stems of callas that enhance the graphic nature of the finished composition. Narrow foliages wrapped intermittently across the frame further enhance the modern effect (Figure 4-14).

III. Grapevine Accents

This wreath is designed on a natural grapevine wreath base. The earthy quality of the grapevine is most compatible with informal garden flowers such as the lilies and bells-of-Ireland used here.

Tape three 22-gauge floral wires with brown tape (stem wrap). Weave the wires through the grapevine to attach the wreath to an easel at the top and farther down on the front legs. Attach a large domed floral-foam cage with additional brown-taped wires to the top left quadrant of the wreath. Attach a smaller domed floral-foam cage to the bottom right quadrant.

Figure 4-14. Contemporary square.

Lightly green each cage with "woodland" foliages, such as huckleberry and ivy. Place lilies to establish a primary focal point in the top cage. Create a secondary focal point with lilies in the lower cage. Arrange bells-of-Ireland, *Leptospermum* or other linear flowers in each cage following the lines of the wreath. Add fillers as desired to enhance the whimsical, nature-inspired feeling of the design (Figure 4-15).

Figure 4-15. Grapevine accents.

Ready-made forms make creating sympathy tributes quicker and easier than cutting the desired shapes from floral foam or plastic foam. Floral-foam forms, which generally feature either plastic or mâché backs, are commonly available in solid and open hearts, double hearts, crosses, rounds, ovals and squares. Specialty shapes, such as "cause ribbons" and irregularly shaped hearts, also are available in floral foam.

Plastic-foam forms, too, are fabricated in all of the most common shapes for sympathy tributes, but there are many more specialty shapes, including emblems for fraternal organizations; spoked wheels and broken-spoke wheels; horseshoes; bibles; stars; pillows; letters and numbers; and even classic, regional favorites like "gates ajar" or "gates awaiting."
Here are a few examples.

Open heart, floral foam

Solid heart, floral foam

Contemporary solid heart, floral foam

Contemporary open heart, floral foam

Square, floral foam

Oval, floral foam

Cross, floral foam

Ribbon, floral foam

Mason (Freemason) emblem, plastic foam

Broken wheel, plastic foam

Shriners emblem, plastic foam

Star, Order of the Eastern Star emblem, plastic foam

Images of OASIS® Floral Foam Mâché Products from Smithers-Oasis; STYROFOAM® brand plastic-foam forms from FloraCraft Corporation.

SYMPATHY CROSS

Crosses are traditional symbols requested for funeral and memorial services. They are most often designed on easels but also can be laid across a casket lid or featured upright in arrangements. Floral-foam crosses are available that allow these arrangements to be designed much like the wreaths described previously. The example that follows uses a plastic-foam cross to demonstrate the mechanics for this type of base.

SUGGESTED MATERIALS

2-3 bunches cushion spray mums (pompons)

10 tulips

7 stems heather

1-2 stems Italian *Pittosporum*

1-2 stems Italian *Ruscus*

#40-width ribbon (optional)

Plastic-foam cross

Domed floral-foam cage

Dixon® pins or greening pins

Floral adhesive

Toothpicks

DESIGN STEPS

Apply floral adhesive to the back of a domed floral-foam cage, and place it in the center of the cross. Insert Dixon® pins or greening pins through the tabs on the cage for added security.

Clip the cushion mums from their stems directly underneath the blooms. Sort the blooms by size.

For Step 3, to attach the cushion mums, choose one of the two following methods.

Method A: Apply flowers to the edges of the cross first, using the smallest blooms. Apply a drop of floral adhesive to the center underside of each blossom, where the stem was attached, and press each flower onto the cross, creating neat rows.

Method B: Cut toothpicks in half and apply floral adhesive to the tips. Insert the toothpicks through the centers of the blooms and into the foam. Cover the top surface of the cross with the largest mums using the same technique, working around the caged foam.

4

Push the backside of the cross downward onto the hook of a wire easel. Secure the cross to the front easel legs by applying floral adhesive to the tips of Dixon® or greening pins and inserting them around the legs and into the back of the cross.

5

Establish a strong diagonal line from upper left to lower right by inserting heather stems securely into the floral-foam cage.

6

Arrange tulips in a crescent line, in the opposite direction, that extends to or even below the base of the cross, to counterbalance the diagonal line.

Optional

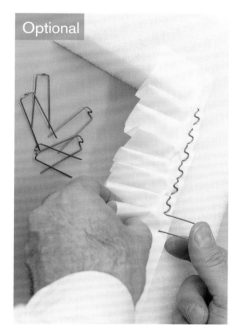

Optional: Create a ruffled ribbon edge around all sides of the cross by gathering and pinning #40 satin ribbon to the back side of the cross before starting Step 1. Make sure to position the ribbon so the shiny side faces the front side of the cross.

7

Enhance the diagonal line and the focal area with Italian Ruscus and Italian *Pittosporum*.

VARIATIONS

Many variations in the cross design can be achieved with minor changes in the design process. To modify the look of the cross described previously, try one of these variations.

I. Hogarth Accent

Follow Steps 1-4 on Pages 82-83, then arrange flowers and foliages that can be curved to form a gentle "S"-shaped Hogarth curve across the center. The top of the "S" should be one-third the total length and the bottom should be two-thirds of the total.

II. Leaf-Covered Cross

Pin or glue individual *Galax* or salal leaves to the top and sides of the cross, overlapping the base of one leaf with the tip of the next. Add a vertical floral accent such as the *Cymbidium* orchid focal point shown here (Figure 4-16).

III. Moss-Covered Cross

Attach sheet moss to the top and sides of a plastic-foam wreath form with greening pins or glue. Add decorative bindings of tied bear grass or pinned lily grass, or colored spool wire, if desired, to help hold the moss in place. Add a floral accent in a diagonal or crescent pattern.

IV. Palm Background

Trim emerald palm to taper the leaves. Attach the palm to the back of the cross with greening pins, extending the outline of the cross in each direction. Add four to six more pieces of palm on angles extending from behind the center of the cross.

V. Branch Cross

Attach a rectangular floral-foam-filled cage vertically to an easel. Arrange birch branches, ti leaves and/or river cane into the top, bottom and sides of the foam cage to form the cross. Green the center of the foam cage, and add a fresh-flower accent (Figure 4-17).

Figure 4-16. Leaf-covered cross.

Figure 4-17. Branch cross.

SET PIECES

Set pieces are symbolic forms that are completely covered in floral materials. These symbols typically represent something important to the deceased such as a hobby or career. Historically significant set piece styles include harps, lyres, anchors, horseshoes, teardrops and broken wheels. In some parts of the United States, these styles remain popular. (For examples, see Page 80.) Modern set pieces include shapes such as musical notes, animals, automobile logos and team mascots.

Usually placed on easels, set pieces are typically designed on plastic-foam bases that are carved into the desired shape or symbol. Some popular symbols, such as the Eastern Star and Rotary emblems, are available ready-made. In addition, sheets of floral foam can be sculpted into original forms.

The process for designing set pieces mirrors that of the cross described on Pages 81-83. Flowers and/or foliage, plus ribbon edgings, are pinned or glued onto plastic-foam bases. Short-stemmed flowers are inserted into floral-foam bases. The goal is to place the flowers neatly, using color to help achieve the look of the object or symbol portrayed by the design (Figure 4-18).

Figure 4-18. Heart-shaped set piece.

1. Use only your freshest flowers. Although sympathy flowers aren't valued for long vase life, arrangements must often stand at room temperature for as long as 48 hours until all services are concluded. If you use fading flowers in your sympathy pieces, that will be evident to both families and funeral directors.

2. Don't be a drip. Designs created in floral-foam forms that drip when displayed upright can create problems for funeral directors, including stained carpets. The best solution is to set arrangements upright in your shop for a few hours, so excess water can be eliminated. Although plastic-foam forms alleviate the dripping problem, funeral directors prefer arrangements with water sources so flowers look their best for the duration of the services.

3. Create balanced designs. Another reason to set sympathy pieces upright in your shop is to ensure proper balance so nothing topples over in the funeral home or at the service. Make certain that all your floral designs, including easels, are stable and will sit or stand securely.

4. Eliminate exposed sharp points. Funeral directors realize that florists often have to use wire and sharp-pointed picks to create their designs. But since sympathy pieces are often moved several times, sharp points can be hazardous to funeral directors. Make sure that sharp picks or wire ends are not exposed.

5. Learn hearse dimensions. Casket sprays are frequently left atop caskets when they're placed into hearses. Many of today's hearses, however, have only 6 to 8 inches of clearance above caskets, so sprays that are too high or mounded often don't fit. If another car is required to transport casket pieces, it is more costly for funeral directors and, sometimes, families, too.

6. Consider size. Excessively large floral pieces are often difficult to display in funeral-home settings whereas smaller pieces can be displayed in more areas and can be taken home by family members and friends after the services. Likewise, potted plants are often welcomed by family members as lasting remembrances.

7. Notify funeral directors of unusual designs. If families request large or unusual pieces, funeral directors will appreciate knowing about these arrangements in advance. Inform them ahead of time of sympathy pieces that might need special care or other accommodations.

8. Deliver early. Funeral directors try to have everything in place long before families arrive, so deliver flowers to funeral homes or service sites at least two hours before the families are scheduled to be there (the amount of time may vary from one funeral home to another, so always know the funeral directors' preferences). Last-minute deliveries of flowers, or deliveries of flowers during visitation or services, make display difficult, if not impossible. Always deliver flowers from family members first so they can be positioned closest to the casket.

9. Make the call. Early deliveries are preferable to late ones, so if you need to make a late-evening delivery the night before a service, call ahead. Funeral directors, who typically have rooms that can be left open for flower deliveries, will be happy to make accommodations, but they need to be notified in advance.

10. Be courteous. Fostering good relationships with funeral directors is valuable to both your business and the families you serve. Often, avoiding these pitfalls requires only a little common courtesy, which goes a long way. Keep the funeral directors' needs in mind, and if you're not sure, ask. Funeral directors will always appreciate your willingness to help them better serve their clients.

V

WEDDING BOUQUETS

Wedding bouquets represent some of the most intricate work that designers create. They require precise mechanics and careful attention to detail as well as keen consideration of proportion, balance and color harmony. Wedding bouquets can be designed in a wide variety of shapes and styles. The bouquets featured in this chapter represent styles that are classics as well as those that follow the current trends in wedding flowers. Once these styles are mastered, the designer will have the skills necessary to expand into the variations described or into a wealth of free-form bouquet possibilities.

ROUND BOUQUET

The round bouquet is a classic style. The familiarity of the circular outline and semispherical form makes it a popular bouquet choice for brides and bridesmaids alike. The keys to making an appealing round bouquet are to maintain an even circular edge and domed top. Flower combinations can range from simple monobotanical compositions (using only one flower type) to *tussie-mussie*-inspired bouquets comprising a plethora of herbs and garden flowers.

Typically created in a foam bouquet holder, this style can be designed to face upward (using a straight-handled bouquet holder) or forward (using a slant-handled bouquet holder). The upward-facing style is much like a low domed version of the round centerpiece described in Chapter II, on Pages 23-25. The bouquet shown here follows the classic format of facing the flowers forward for maximum impact during the processional and recessional and in wedding-day photographs.

SUGGESTED MATERIALS

9 roses

7-9 Freesias

3-4 stems button spray mums (pompons)

3-5 stems *Hypericum*

3-5 stems leatherleaf fern

1-2 stems ming fern

Slant-handled foam bouquet holder

2-3 yards #9-width ribbon

DESIGN STEPS

1 Soak the floral-foam bouquet holder in properly prepared flower-food solution. Establish the circular outline of the bouquet by inserting three 4"-long leatherleaf fern tips around the edge of the foam in a "Y" shape.

2 Add three more leatherleaf fern tips in the spaces between the original three. Check the side view to be sure each stem is perpendicular to the foam cage, following the slanted angle of the bouquet holder.

3 Green the center of the bouquet holder by adding slightly shorter tips of leatherleaf fern into the flat, top surface of the foam in a radiating pattern, extending from the center outward.

4 Cut three roses to a length of 4½" - 5". Insert these roses about 1" into the foam near the center of the bouquet holder to establish the focal area. The roses should be positioned in a moderately spaced zigzag pattern to avoid looking like a pyramid or two eyes and a nose. The roses should face outward on different angles, with the top rose facing slightly upward, the center rose facing slightly to the side and the bottom rose facing slightly downward.

5 Arrange three more roses into the outer edge of the foam bouquet holder so that they form the letter "Y" and follow the slanted angle of the holder.

6 Arrange the remaining three roses around the edge of the bouquet holder in the spaces between the three roses placed in the previous step.

7

Cut individual button mums from the main stem, and distribute them in a radiating pattern between the roses. Allow a moderate amount of variation in stem length to create depth in the bouquet. Be sure that some of the centrally placed button mums have enough length to create the desired dome shape. This will be most evident when checking the bouquet from the side.

8

Insert stems of ming fern to add softness and further define the dome shape.

9

Arrange the *Freesias* in spaces throughout the design.

10

Tuck clusters of *Hypericum* into any remaining spaces in the design.

11

Add ribbon, and finish the handle and the back of the bouquet as desired. (See Pages 102; 104-106; 109-111.)

VARIATIONS

I. Collared Monobotanical Bouquet

Bouquets designed with a single flower type are sometimes referred to as "monobotanical." When tightly spaced and surrounded by a strong foliage or ribbon collar, the resulting form has an appealing sense of geometry. To design such a bouquet, it is not necessary to first green the bouquet holder. Instead, start with a round outline of flowers (such as miniature carnations) placing the individual blossoms close together. Then, develop the center of the bouquet as described in Step 4, but with little or no space between the flowers. Fill out the semisphere with flowers placed close to one another, adding buds among the fully open flowers for contrast.

Use broadleaf foliage, such as salal or *Galax* leaves, to develop an even collar around the bouquet, or use ribbon loops or tulle puffs for a softer edge. Some foliages can be inserted directly into the foam bouquet holder; others must be wired prior to insertion. Here, wired salal leaves are dressed with lace ribbon glued in place with spray adhesive and trimmed along each leaf outline. To maintain an even circular shape, all of the leaves should be a consistent size. A few leaves added into the center of the bouquet add contrast and strengthen the unity of the finished composition (Figure 5-1).

II. Cloud Bouquet

The cloud bouquet is characterized by a round mass of baby's breath or other light floral filler (*Limonium*, waxflowers, etc.), with an understory of flowers whose colors peek through the "cloud." To create this style, begin by arranging a simple collar of greens around a foam bouquet holder; then add a concentrated mass of flowers in a small dome shape across the foam. Arrange baby's breath or other filler flowers to a height twice that of the flowers. Continue adding the filler across the top and around the sides of the bouquet holder until a full round shape is formed (Figure 5-2).

III. Teardrop Bouquet

The teardrop bouquet is a round bouquet that dips to a point at the base (Figure 5-3). The dip extends the bouquet slightly but not with the formality and drama of a complete cascade. The point of the teardrop can be formed by flowers, foliage, ribbon or accessories. The top of the bouquet can be smoothly rounded or more loosely formed as long as the focal point is strong and the shape is balanced.

To create the teardrop bouquet shown here, establish an outline of *Magnolia* leaves, placing the longest leaves at the base. Cluster roses in the center, using the "Y" pattern for initial insertions. Carry the rose placements from the center to the edges. Elongate the center line and emphasize the teardrop shape with ribbon streamers.

Figure 5-1. Collared monobotanical bouquet.

Figure 5-2. Baby's breath cloud bouquet.

Figure 5-3. Teardrop bouquet.

CASCADE BOUQUET

Cascade bouquets are characterized by long extensions of flowers that drape (or "cascade") downward from the central bouquet in a variety of ways. The traditional cascade bouquet is a symmetrical style that has a dramatic flowing line of flowers down the center. This formal style is often the bouquet of choice for brides seeking to make dramatic entrances on their wedding days.

Mechanics for cascade bouquets vary, but since these designs typically involve more flowers than round bouquets, extra-large bouquet holders are often used to support the many stem insertions. Both straight-handled and slant-handled bouquet holders can be used to create cascade bouquets. Some designers prefer the fullness that comes from designing a cascade bouquet in a straight-handled holder. With this mechanic, it is often easier for a bride to hold the bouquet without the weight of the cascading flowers pulling the design forward and off balance. However, when attempting the cascade style for the first time, most designers find slant-handled holders easier to master. For this reason, a slant-handled holder is used here.

SUGGESTED MATERIALS

10 roses	¼-⅓ bunch heather
4-5 stems spray (miniature) carnations	4-5 stems leatherleaf fern
1-3 stems *Godetia*	2-3 stems seeded *Eucalyptus*
lily buds	Extra-large slant-handled bouquet holder

DESIGN STEPS

1 Insert three leatherleaf fern tips into the bouquet holder in a "Y" formation.

2 Arrange three more 3" - 4" tips of leatherleaf fern between the first three placements.

3 Green the center of the bouquet holder by adding slightly shorter tips of leatherleaf fern into the flat, top surface of the foam in a radiating pattern.

4 Insert a long stem of heather into the bottom edge of the bouquet holder. Add support if needed (see Pages 99-101).

5 Add a slightly shorter stem of heather on both sides of the first stem. Strive for a subtle stair-step pattern.

6 Insert two shorter stems of heather into the top back edge of the bouquet holder to form a "V." These stems should arch back slightly.

7 Add similar-sized pieces of heather in evenly spaced placements around the edge.

8 Arrange additional pieces of heather into the top, flat surface of the foam, radiating from the center to fill out the design.

9 Place two stems of *Godetia* into the center of the bouquet holder.

Place one more *Godetia* below the original grouping to fill out the focal area of the bouquet.

Arrange three roses to radiate from the same central point as the *Godetias*. One rose should look to 11 o'clock, another to 4 o'clock, and the third to 7 o'clock.

Place another rose extending downward vertically so that its head falls between the bottom-most *Godetia* and the tip of the longest heather stem.

Position two roses in the back edge of the bouquet holder, above the focal flowers, to form a "V."

Arrange the remaining four roses to round out the edges of the bouquet and create a rose outline between the top of the bouquet and the cascade.

Arrange miniature carnations throughout the bouquet, using open blossoms near the center and buds at the edges. Check the bouquet from the side to assess the development of depth and a mounded form.

Arrange lily buds to follow the shape of the design. Secure two buds into the cascade portion of the bouquet. Add seeded *Eucalyptus* lightly throughout.

VARIATIONS

I. Monochromatic Cascade

The traditional cascade bouquet is often designed with a combination of flower forms and flower colors. The monochromatic variation uses only one color to achieve its look. In this bouquet, the round *Scabiosas* provide a full design form with a neatly manicured appearance that is well suited to many bridal and bridesmaid gowns. Another option for this form is a monobotanical variation, using just one flower type.

To create the monochromatic example shown, minimize the foliage used to green the bouquet holder. Establish a strong focal area, then stagger several additional flowers down the center line of the bouquet to achieve the desired cascade length. Form a curved top much like that of a round bouquet, then fill out the cascade. Here, a few pale blue-violet *Delphiniums* are used as the unifying element among the many lavender *Scabiosas* and *Guichenotias* (Figure 5-4).

II. Crescent Bouquet

The crescent bouquet is an asymmetrical variation. Instead of a central cascading line, this bouquet features an arching line that flows through the center of the bouquet, from one side to the other (Figure 5-5). The center vertical line, filled with flowers in a traditional cascade, is vacant.

Select flowers and foliages with naturally curved stems or that can be manipulated into curved shapes. Develop the design outline with lily grass or other curved foliage that arches to the left at the 9 o'clock or 8 o'clock position and to the right at the 3 o'clock or 4 o'clock position. The shape should taper from narrow tips at each side of the bouquet to a center that is slightly broader than the bouquet holder.

Arrange a trio of flowers into the center of the bouquet holder to establish the focal area. Stagger placements of two or three more of the focal flower toward the left tip of the bouquet.

Establish each tip of the crescent with two or three stems of line flowers. Broaden the center of the design with a second flower type that extends above and below the focal flowers. Disperse this flower type toward each side of the bouquet to unify the tips with the center. Expand the flower and foliage mix, as desired, to increase the texture and interest.

III. Waterfall Bouquet

The waterfall bouquet has the same general shape as a traditional cascade bouquet, with a rounded top flowing to a tapered central tip. What makes a waterfall bouquet distinctive is the forward-flowing rhythm and the layering of the materials. In this style, the traditional radial rhythm (in which flowers emerge from the center outward in all directions) is replaced by parallel rhythm, with flowers flowing forward and cascading downward side by side (Figure 5-6). Use a variety of flower and foliage forms and textures to create interest among the layers.

To create a waterfall bouquet, start with a straight-handled bouquet holder. Collar the holder with broadleaf foliage such as *Galax* leaves. Begin designing at the front edge of the holder with pliable, linear foliages, such as lily grass, ivy or plumosa fern, shaped and positioned to form a dramatic drop. Add two or more impact flowers, such as callas, orchids or *Gerberas*, into the focal area, and extend one or more of these flowers into the cascade. Accent the impact flower with a secondary flower positioned so blossoms flow parallel to one another from the back of the holder through the focal area and into the cascade.

Create another layer of linear foliages (lily grass, ivy or plumosa fern) that flows from behind the focal area, over the central flowers and down into the cascade. Add filler flowers, as desired, following the same layered pattern and parallel rhythm. Repeat the flowing lines with ribbon, yarn, spool wire or bullion wire. Beads, gems, mirror chips or other decorative items are also desirable additions for texture and interest.

Figure 5-4. Monochromatic cascade.

Figure 5-5. Crescent bouquet.

Figure 5-6. Waterfall bouquet.

HAND-TIED BOUQUET

Hand-tied bouquets are characterized by a collection of flowers that appear gathered, as if freshly picked from the garden. The handles of these bouquets are formed by the stems of the flowers; therefore, there is no need for foam bouquet holders or other mechanical aids.

There are a number of ways to assemble the flowers into a hand-tied bouquet. These methods include creating a network of foliages and/or filler flowers into which the other flowers are threaded, spiraling the flowers around one another, and binding small clusters of flowers into a larger mass bouquet. The method demonstrated here, which relies on a base of sturdy flowers to support the subsequent flower additions, is one of the simplest to master. Note, however, that practice is the key to success with hand-tied bouquets. If one method is a challenge, try another.

SUGGESTED MATERIALS

3 stems *Hydrangeas*

7 carnations

6-8 stocks

6-8 *Freesias*

3-5 stems spray roses

8-10 stems salal leaves

Waterproof tape, wax string, raffia
  or a zip tie

2-3 yards #9-width ribbon

DESIGN STEPS

1 Strip all foliage and thorns from the lower ⅔ to ¾ of all stems of flowers before beginning. Cluster three stems of *Hydrangeas*, holding them 2" - 3" below the blossoms.

2 Insert three carnations in between the *Hydrangea* blossoms so the bases of the carnations are nestled among the *Hydrangeas*. Form a loose grip around the flowers, using your thumb and index finger.

3 Evenly distribute the remaining four carnations around the edge of the bouquet in a round shape, with stems positioned at 45-degree angles. These angles will help to provide the desired domed bouquet form.

4 Arrange three stocks among the carnations in the center of the bouquet. To avoid snapping the stems during insertion, keep a loose grip around the bouquet. Watch from beneath the bouquet to determine where the stock stems begin to emerge, then grasp the stem ends and pull the stocks in to the depth desired.

5 Evenly distribute the remaining stocks between the carnations at the edge of the bouquet. Position the stems at 45-degree angles. Add enough stems to complete a round outline.

6 Add *Freesias* throughout the bouquet by threading stems through the center of the bouquet and positioning the flowers at angles around the bouquet's edge.

Tuck spray roses among the other flowers, as needed, to complete the rounded dome and accent the bouquet.

Add a collar of salal leaves to the underside of the bouquet by positioning each leaf base where the bouquet is gripped in the hand (the binding point) and overlapping the leaf edges.

Bind the bouquet with waterproof tape (or wax string, raffia or a zip tie), wrapping the tape, string, raffia or tie three or four times above the grip of the hand.

Trim the stem ends to about 4" - 5". For a freestanding bouquet, cut the center stems ½" shorter than the outer stems.

Cover the tape binding with ribbon or other decorative material, as desired.

VARIATIONS

I. Rose Clutch Bouquet

A clutch bouquet is quite simply a fistful of flowers bound into a single unit. Often monobotanical, these bouquets can be made large or small. For a simple rose clutch, begin with a single, partially open rose, and surround it with five more roses so that the flower heads all touch one another. Add a simple collar of foliage such as *Galax* leaves beneath the blooms, and bind the stems above the fist that clutches the flowers with waterproof tape, floral tape, wax string or raffia.

For a larger rose clutch (Figure 5-7), start with three roses grouped together, and surround this trio with six or more roses. The more roses that are used, the more the depth of the flower placements can be varied, with some roses tucked in deep and others extending into a rounded outline. Add foliage, such as sprengeri fern, to soften the edge, and add a ribbon accent as desired.

II. Scepter Bouquet

Another hand-tied bouquet variation features an extended bouquet handle of natural flower stems that yields a simple scepter-style design (Figure 5-8). Many flowers, such as roses, tulips, lilies, *Alstroemerias, Amaryllises,* callas and even carnations can be used for this bouquet. A single flower type, such as the *Gerberas* used here, is generally more effective than a mixed combination.

Choose flowers with long stems, and remove all leaves and thorns from each stem. Evenly arrange all of the flower heads close together. Bind the stems just below the blooms. Align the stems into a tight, neat staff, and bind them again near the base. Wrap ribbon starting near the base of the stems up the stems, adding a flourish of loops or streamers, as desired, at the top.

III. Filler Bouquet

For this bouquet, a base of fluffy filler flowers or foliage, such as baby's breath or ming fern, becomes the base through which the other filler flowers are inserted. At the beginning of the design process, the filler base dominates, but as the design progresses, the filler eventually becomes a background to the flower clusters. The size of the finished bouquet is determined by the size of the filler base.

To begin, strip all of the foliage from the lower portion of all flower stems. Clutch several stems of baby's breath, ming fern or other filler to form a loosely rounded mass. Holding the clutch of filler in one hand, insert three or more filler flower clusters into the center. Continue adding filler clusters around the focal clusters, making sure to shift the angles of insertion so that the outermost clusters are threaded through on the sharpest angles. Add foliage, as needed, around the outer edge of the bouquet; bind with waterproof tape, floral tape, wax string or raffia; and cover the binding with a simple ribbon accent (Figure 5-9).

Figure 5-7. Rose clutch bouquet.

Figure 5-8. Simple scepter bouquet.

Figure 5-9. Filler bouquet.

SPECIAL BOUQUET MECHANICS

Wedding bouquets are special designs that often require special mechanics. Because bouquets receive a great deal of handling, flowers designed in floral-foam bouquet holders sometimes require extra procedures to make sure they remain secure in the bouquets. Accessories are sometimes desired to enhance and personalize bouquets. Backings are always necessary to cover mechanics and give the bouquets a finished quality. Bouquet handles also may warrant special treatments to add length, soften stems or enhance their decorative appeal. Utilize the following techniques to make bouquets that not only look good but also hold up well throughout the wedding day.

SECURING STEMS

When designing bouquets in floral-foam bouquet holders, stems sometimes need extra support during and/or after insertion. A variety of mechanical aids can help provide security.

Wood Picks

Soft-stemmed flowers, such as *Ranunculi*, can be difficult to insert. Attaching a **wired wood pick** near the base of the stem makes it easier to push the stem into place.

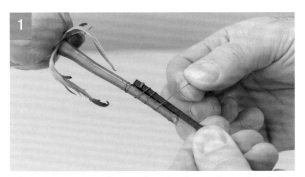

Align a 2½" wired wood pick along the side of the flower stem near the base. Wrap the wire around the flower stem, above the wood pick, two or three times; then wrap it around both the stem and pick two or three times; and finish by wrapping the rest of the wire around the pick alone, below the stem.

Insert the pick and stem into the bouquet holder, making sure the base of the flower stem comes in contact with the foam.

Hollow-stemmed flowers, such as daffodils, sometimes bend or break when being inserted into floral foam. In this case, small unwired wood picks or chenille stems can be inserted into the ends of the stems to provide firmness and ease insertion into the bouquet holder (Figures 5-10 and 5-11).

Thick-stemmed flowers, such as callas, sometimes make large holes in the foam when inserted into bouquet holders. This makes the flowers more susceptible to falling out, especially when the flowers are in a cascading position. To increase the security of these flowers, impale each flower stem with a **2½-inch unwired wood pick** or **toothpick** to hold the stem in place. Insert each stem into the bouquet holder, then insert a wooden pick into the foam, through each stem, and out the other side of the foam (Figure 5-12). The pick should be perpendicular to the stem. In other words, if the stem is inserted horizontally, the pick should be inserted vertically, and vice versa.

Figures 5-10 and 5-11. Inserting a chenille stem, left, or a wood pick, right, into a daffodil stem.

Figure 5-12. Impaling a calla stem with a wood pick.

Glues

Sometimes flowers in foam bouquet holders need a little boost to ensure they will stay in place with heavy handling. A variety of glues can be used to help give stems extra holding power.

Liquid floral adhesive is a glue specially formulated for use on flowers. To use this glue, apply a liberal amount to the sides of the flower stem near the base. Insert the stem into the bouquet holder. Within a minute or two, the glue will become tacky and provide notable support. Because there is no glue on the stem end, the flower can still draw water from the wet foam (Figure 5-13).

Small, lightweight flowers, such as individual *Delphinium, Agapanthus* or hyacinth florets are sometimes difficult to use in bouquets because they lack stem length. **Hot glues**, from either a glue gun or a hot-melt glue pan; **cool-melt glue**; or **liquid floral adhesive** can be used to provide a quick stick when these blossoms are placed among other flowers already arranged into the foam. A small dot of glue is usually all that is needed to make the short-stemmed blossoms hold their positions within the design (Figure 5-14).

Figure 5-13. Floral adhesive applied to the sides of a flower stem.

Figure 5-14. Floral adhesive applied to the stem of an individual blossom. Hot-melt and cool-melt glues also can be used.

To add security to an entire finished bouquet, **spray floral adhesives** provide a means of holding multiple stems firmly in position. To use a spray floral adhesive on a finished bouquet, attach the small straw provided with the product to the spray nozzle. Insert the straw into the center of the bouquet until it makes contact with the foam. Spray a small amount of adhesive against the foam; then move the straw to a new position, and repeat until all insertion points have been sprayed (Figure 5-15). Allow the adhesive to dry completely before the bouquet is used.

Figure 5-15. Spray floral adhesive applied to a finished bouquet.

Wires

Cascade bouquets with many long stems flowing from the base of a floral-foam bouquet holder can cause concern about stem security. **Wire** can be used to lock these stems into position. Cut the flower to the desired length. Tape a wire (usually 22-gauge or 24-gauge wire is ideal). Wrap the middle of the wire around the lower 2 inches of stem. Insert the ends of the wire into the bouquet holder until the flower's stem end is deep within the foam. The wire ends will emerge through the top of the bouquet holder where they can be twisted together around a plastic rib of the bouquet cage to lock the flower into place. Trim the ends of the wires close to the bouquet holder (Figure 5-16).

Figure 5-16. Securing a flower stem into a bouquet holder with taped wire.

Some flowers need support to prevent premature wilting or to provide added length. Wiring these flowers can solve both problems. For flowers with adequate stem length, insert a wire into the base of the blossom and gently wrap the wire around the stem in a downward spiral, then insert it into the foam (Figure 5-17). For flowers that need added length, use the wiring techniques described in Chapter III, Pages 37-43, but choose a wire gauge based on the individual flower positions (lightweight wire for cascading flowers; medium- to heavy-gauge wire for upright placements).

Figure 5-17. Wiring a flower stem for added support.

Typically, wired flowers are taped with floral tape (stem wrap) before use. *Stephanotises* sometimes are an exception when commercially available "*Stephanotis* stems" are used as a wiring alternative (see Chapter III, Page 40). However, when *Stephanotis* stems need to be extended with wire, such as when placed into a cascade bouquet, these stems usually are taped as well. The addition of short wired wood picks to the ends of thin wire stems is a common practice. The square wood picks won't twist when inserted into the wet floral foam, and they also will swell, making them less prone to falling out than thin wires without wood picks attached (Figure 5-18).

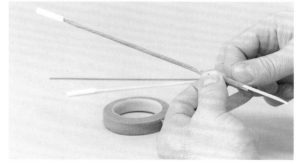

Figure 5-18. Taping a wood pick to a "Stephanotis stem."

Accessories often make an ordinary bouquet more special. These details provide an excellent means of accentuating a color scheme or otherwise personalizing a bouquet to a bride. Some of the most popular bouquet accessories are described here, along with mechanics for their use.

Bows and Streamers

Bows are a common finishing touch for bouquets. There are many ways to create bows, some of which are described in Chapter III, on Pages 44-48. The **traditional florist bow** suits many round bouquets when positioned at the front lip of the design. For this application, the bow can be wired and taped to a wood pick, and inserted like a flower placement (Figure 5-19).

Sometimes, a traditional florist bow can overpower a bouquet or disrupt its shape. In this case, a simpler **"shoestring" bow**, with two loops and two streamers, can be wired and taped to a wood pick and inserted into the bouquet (Figure 5-20).

Occasionally, a collection of **loops on individual picks** provides a bowlike appearance without the mass of ribbon created by a complete bow. (Figure 5-21).

Streamers are another effective method of using ribbon in bouquets. Whether or not a bow is used, several lengths of ribbon can be gathered in the center of each piece and wired and taped to a wood pick. To place streamers into a hand-tied bouquet, the wood pick should be replaced by taped wire or a length of ribbon that can be tied onto the cluster of stems.

A shoestring bow can be attached to a hand-tied bouquet at its binding point with taped wire (Figure 5-22) or ribbon (Figure 5-23).

Figure 5-19. A traditional florist bow wired and taped to a wood pick for insertion into a floral-foam bouquet holder.

Figure 5-20. A "shoestring bow" wired and taped to a wood pick for insertion into a floral-foam bouquet holder.

Figure 5-21. Individual loops wired and taped to wood picks for insertion into a floral-foam bouquet holder.

Figure 5-22. Wiring a "shoestring bow" to a hand-tied bouquet's binding point with taped wire.

Figure 5-23. Tying a "shoestring bow" to a hand-tied bouquet's binding point with ribbon.

Pearls, Beads and Jewels

Corsage pins provide another means of incorporating decorative accents into bouquets. Traditional pearl-headed corsage pins and other gem-tipped pins are available in a variety of colors that, when used singly or in clusters, add contrast and interest to individual flowers and bouquets. Larger decorative bead or gem pins as well as ornate hat pins can be inserted between flowers for added effect (Figure 5-24).

Rhinestone, pearl and other **jeweled sprays** sometimes are wired and taped onto wired wood picks to make insertion into bouquets as simple as the flower placements (Figure 5-25). Loose pearls, beads and jewels can be glued into the centers or throats of individual flowers.

Decorative spool wire or **jewelry wire** can be used to thread through individual beads to make bead strands (Figure 5-26) or clusters for incorporation into bouquets.

Figure 5-24. Jewel-headed pins placed into the centers of roses.

Figure 5-25. Jewel sprays wired and taped to a wood pick for insertion into a bouquet.

Figure 5-26. Beads threaded onto decorative wire to create strands for incorporation into bouquets.

For a different look, **beads** can be positioned intermittently along a strand of decorative wire. This technique involves threading each bead into the desired position along the wire, then threading the wire through the bead a second time to hold it in place (Figure 5-27).

Individual pearls, beads and jewels are popular accessories for dressing up wedding bouquets. These decorative accessories are often available on pins or wire stems that either can be arranged between the flowers or placed in the centers or throats of the individual flowers in a bouquet. For jewels without pins attached, simply adhere with a drop of floral adhesive (Figure 5-28).

Figure 5-27. Positioning beads intermittently along a strand of decorative wire.

Figure 5-28. Jewels incorporated into a bouquet with floral adhesive.

Just as the back of a one-sided flower arrangement should be finished with foliage, wedding bouquets should be finished on the back or underside so that none of the mechanics can be seen. A variety of creative methods can be employed to complete this important detail. Sometimes the backing is established at the beginning of the design process while other times, the backing is added at the end. Several versatile backing methods are presented here for use with a variety of bouquet styles.

Bouquet Collars

Bouquet collars of lace, satin and tulle are manufactured to slide up the handle of a bouquet holder and snap into place underneath the floral-foam cage. The flanges at the base of these collars can be taped to the bouquet-holder handle, or they can be removed altogether. When taped into place, the tape must be covered with ribbon. When the flanges are removed, the raw edge of the collar must be covered.

Backing a bouquet holder with a lace collar

Slide the handle of a bouquet holder into the center of a manufactured bouquet collar.

Tape the collar into place, and tie a satin ribbon bow to cover the mechanics of the bouquet collar attachment. Glue the bow into place.

Backing a bouquet holder with a foliage-covered lace collar

To create a collar of leaves, glue leaves atop the lace of a manufactured bouquet collar.

Continue gluing leaves to the collar, overlapping them to complete the circle. Slide the bouquet handle into the collar.

Backing bouquet holders with tulle poufs or satin bows

An alternative to the manufactured bouquet collar is to attach poufs of tulle or ribbon bows around the base of the bouquet (Figure 5-29). This technique can be used for both hand-tied bouquets and styles designed in bouquet holders. Depending on their size, typically three to five poufs or bows will be needed for an average bouquet.

Figure 5-29. Tulle poufs or bows can be used to cover the back or underside of a bouquet.

To create **tulle poufs**, follow these instructions. For bow-making instructions, see Chapter III, Pages 45-46.

Loop tulle back and forth as if creating a bow, making all of the loops approximately the same size (as opposed to the varying sizes typically used for a traditional florist bow). The number of loops and their size can be adjusted depending on the size of the bouquet and the fullness desired. An average-size pouf might have six to eight loops on each side, with each loop about 3" - 3½" in length.

Tie the tulle pouf tightly in the center with a taped wire or another piece of tulle, then fluff the loops. (If using taped wire, tape the wire with white tape for bouquet holders and green tape for hand-tied bouquets.) Make enough poufs, three to five, to surround a bouquet or its holder and give the desired fullness.

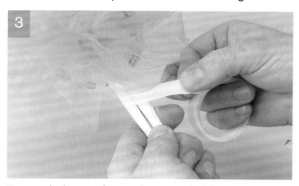

To attach the poufs to a bouquet holder, tape them one at a time to the handle. Tape the wires the entire length of the bouquet handle, and trim, as needed, at the base. Cover the taped handle using one of the techniques described in "Bouquet Handles," Pages 107-111. To attach the poufs to a hand-tied bouquet, place the tulle directly beneath the flowers, and tape the wires to the cluster of stems. Trim the wires below the binding point.

Foliage Backings

Figure 5-30. A bouquet holder backed with foliage inserted, facing outward, into the slots in the back of the holder.

The slots in the back of most floral-foam bouquet holders provide a means for easily finishing the back sides of the bouquets. Many types of foliage, including leatherleaf fern, ming fern, *Galax* leaves and salal leaves, can be used to fill these spaces. When doing so, position the foliage so the front of each leaf or fern frond faces the back of the bouquet, providing a polished view from the back. It is important for the stems used in this position to be kept short enough so that the back side of the foliage is not visible from the front side of the completed bouquet (Figure 5-30).

For greater coverage of the back of a foam bouquet holder, broadleaf foliage, such as *Galax* or salal leaves, can be glued into place before the bouquet is designed (Figure 5-31).

Figure 5-31. A bouquet holder backed with foliage that is glued, facing outward, onto the back of the holder.

Trim the stems completely from each *Galax* leaf. Spray floral adhesive onto the back sides of the leaves.

Lay the bouquet holder upside-down so it rests on the surface of the foam. Position the first leaf with the base at the top of the handle and the tip near the bottom edge of the holder.

Add the next leaves so they overlap the first and wrap around each side of the bouquet holder.

Place the final leaf so it is centered with the base of the leaf at the top of the handle and the tip of the leaf near the top edge of the bouquet holder.

BOUQUET HANDLES

The natural stems of hand-tied bouquets and the plastic handles of floral-foam bouquet holders are both considered acceptable finishes for bouquet handles. However, sometimes a more decorative look or a special effect is desired. For these situations, there are a number of bouquet handle treatments that can be employed.

Hand-Tieds

Hand-tied bouquets can be enhanced with a simple ribbon bow or a series of knotted ties. These are most effective when double-faced satin or sheer ribbon is used. For a **simple bow**, tie the ribbon in the same manner as when tying a shoe. Be sure the center is pulled tight and the loops are rounded. It may be necessary to adjust the loop sizes, making them smaller and then larger again, to get the center completely tightened (Figure 5-32).

To create **knotted ties**, several short pieces of ribbon (about 5 to 7 inches each) are needed. These pieces all can be of the same ribbon, or a whimsical look can be achieved by using pieces of several different ribbons. Starting at the binding point of the bouquet, tie each ribbon around the stem into a knot, with ribbon ends neatly trimmed. Space each ribbon tie an inch or so apart, ending the ties at a point that allows the bouquet to be placed in water without the ribbons getting wet (Figure 5-33).

Figure 5-32. A hand-tied bouquet enhanced with a simple ribbon bow.

Figure 5-33. Knotted ties of ribbon enhance the stem cluster of a hand-tied bouquet.

For a **"French braid,"** use a piece of No. 9-width ribbon that is four times the length of the bouquet handle (see how-to steps below).

Starting at the base of the handle, tie a length of ribbon around the stem cluster, and wrap both ribbon ends around to the back side of the handle. Where the ribbon meets, twist the two pieces around each other and bring each end back to the front.

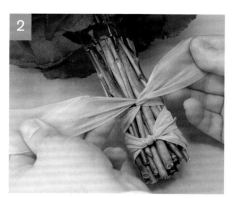

When the ends meet at the front, twist them around each other and wrap them around to the back.

Continue working up to the top of the stem cluster, making sure all the twists are aligned. At the top, tie the remaining ribbon into a bow. Insert a boutonniere pin at an angle to catch the bow and secure it to the stems, keeping the ribbons from loosening. This pin can be placed in the center of the bow for a decorative touch or can be obscured just beneath the bow.

Commercial bouquet wraps provide a simple means for covering the stem clusters of hand-tied bouquets. These decorative satin bands are simply wrapped around the stems and secured with Velcro® fasteners (Figure 5-34).

Figure 5-34. Satin bouquet wrap around a cluster of stems.

A similar finish can be created using wide ribbon (such as No. 40 or No. 100 double-faced satin).

Cut a piece of ribbon approximately 12" long. Apply a line of hot glue along one end of the ribbon, and adhere this end to the stems.

Wrap the ribbon around the stems, overlapping itself at least once before gluing the other end in place and finishing with decorative pins. A #9 or #40 ribbon bow can be tied around the handle wrap, if desired.

To wrap a larger portion of a hand-tied bouquet handle, use No. 9 ribbon. Glue the ribbon near the base of the stem ends, and wrap the ribbon toward the top of the bouquet. Knot the ribbon at the top, and add a pin or dot of glue, if needed, to secure the wrap. (Figure 5-35).

Figure 5-35. Wrapping a hand-tied bouquet handle.

Foam Bouquet Holders

Sometimes, a **hand-tied look** is desired for a bouquet designed in a bouquet holder. To achieve this, begin with a straight, round-handled bouquet holder. Cover the back of the holder by gluing on leaves as described in "Foliage Backings" on Page 106. Design the bouquet, saving all stems that are cut from the flowers during the design process.

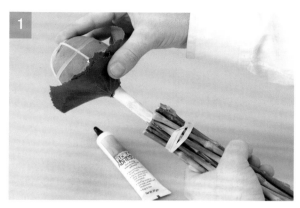

Cluster the saved bouquet stems into a bundle that is flush at one end. Bind the bundle at top and bottom with rubber bands. Apply floral adhesive to the bouquet holder handle, and slide the stem unit onto the handle until it reaches the top. Some of the center stems will be displaced.

Trim the stem ends so they are equal lengths but longer than the bouquet handle.

Remove the rubber bands, and decorate the point where the stems unite with the top of the bouquet holder, and the bottom if desired, with a ribbon wrap or tie to cover the mechanics.

Commercial decorative bouquet holder handles provide an alternative means of dressing handles. These cone-shaped accessories, available in an array of colors and fabrics, instantly dress up bouquet handles. Apply low-temperature glue from a glue gun to the straight handle of a foam bouquet holder. Then, simply slide the decorative cone onto the handle, adding a ribbon tie to cover and unify the connection point (Figure 5-36).

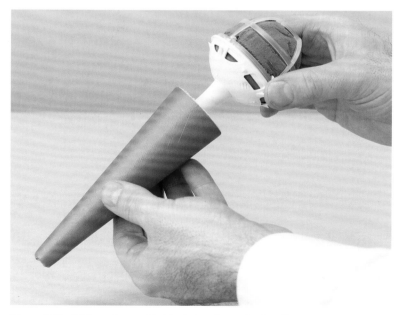

Figure 5-36. Sliding a bouquet holder into a decorative handle.

Ribbon wrapping is a technique that can be used to finish handles of floral-foam bouquet holders.

Cover the bouquet holder handle with double-sided tape.

Starting about 2" from the bottom of the handle, position a piece of #9 ribbon (approximately 1 yard) at a 45-degree angle against the handle.

Wrap the ribbon downward around the handle in an overlapping manner. Continue wrapping beyond the end of the handle.

Flip the excess ribbon up against the handle, and glue into place. Then wrap the ribbon upward around the handle.

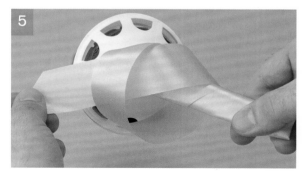

Continue wrapping upward. At the top, form a loop of ribbon, and pull the ribbon end through the loop tightly to knot it.

Add a dot of hot glue to hold the ribbon tie in place, and trim away any excess ribbon.

Bouquet handles can be given a modern look by adding a wandlike extension. To do so, use a straight, round-handled bouquet holder.

Wrap a bouquet holder handle with double-sided tape.

Align hyacinth stakes (about 12) around the handle, with the top of each stake at the top of the handle. Tape the bundle with floral tape (stem wrap), from the top to halfway down the stakes. Trim the stakes to the desired length, and resume taping.

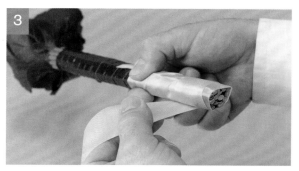

Wrap the hyacinth stake "wand" with ribbon as described on Page 110, eliminating the folded tube of ribbon at the end of the wand.

Wire several lengths of ribbon together in the center. Trim the wires, and put a dot of hot glue where the wire is twisted around the ribbons. Insert the wire ends into the end of the hyacinth stake cluster so that the glue comes into contact with the ends of the stakes.

Trim the ribbon tails to the desired lengths, at a decorative angle.

VI

BALLOONS

Balloons are fun and festive design elements that can be incorporated into flower arrangements or used on their own. There are many types and sizes of balloons, from the traditional round latex balloons to the wide array of character-shaped foil balloons. The term "Mylar," which is a trade name, is sometimes incorrectly used to describe foil balloons. These balloons aren't made of Mylar but rather a combination of nylon film, metallic foil and polyethylene.

INFLATING YOUR SKILLS

Working with balloons requires an under-standing not only of mechanics and design techniques but also environmental and safety considerations that are quite different from working with flowers. For some people, balloon work is intimidating, perhaps due to the inherent possibility of a startling pop. However, with a little basic balloon knowledge and a bit of practice, balloons can be a terrific addition to a floral designer's repertoire.

Balloons are fairly safe products to work with. Other than the potential choking hazard that uninflated or burst latex balloons pose to young children or pets, balloons themselves are not particularly dangerous. On the other hand, helium, the highly pressurized gas used to inflate balloons, is potentially dangerous. In addition, certain environmental factors can affect the potential for balloons to burst or to droop. For these reasons, it is important to understand the safety and environmental factors that affect the process of working with balloons.

Safety Issues

When working with balloons, follow these simple safety precautions:

1. Keep uninflated latex balloons out of reach of young children and pets. Dispose of pieces from burst latex balloons immediately.
2. Keep helium tanks in a well-ventilated area. Avoid using helium in an enclosed space such as a closet.
3. Keep helium tanks away from extreme heat. (Levels above 130 F are dangerous.) Also, keep helium tanks away from sources of electricity.
4. Anchor helium tanks to a permanent fixture such as a wall or counter. Nylon straps or sturdy chains work well for this purpose. Do not remove the valve protector cap until the tank is anchored into place.
5. Keep the helium inflation valve tightly closed between uses.
6. Do not inhale helium. Doing so may cause headaches, dizziness, loss of consciousness and even death.

Environmental Issues

When working with balloons, it is important to be aware of the impact balloons can have on the environment as well as the impact the environment can have on balloons.

Foil balloons are not biodegradable and, therefore, cause concern when released into the environment. Latex balloons, which are manufactured from tree sap, are 100 percent biodegradable and usually will decompose at the same rate as oak leaves. Beyond the issue of biodegradability, balloons released into the environment may pose a variety of dangers to animal life. Some animal protection groups claim that balloons and balloon ribbons ingested by animals can cause serious illness or death. Foil balloons are capable of conducting electricity. In some communities, a single foil balloon caught in electrical lines or an electrical substation reportedly has been the cause of significant power outages. For all of these reasons, it is important to attach weights to all helium-inflated balloons.

Environmental conditions can significantly affect the flotation of helium-filled balloons. Helium is a gas that expands and contracts in response to temperature. Warmth causes expansion of the gas; cold causes contraction. Thus, a balloon inflated to capacity in a cool environment likely will burst if moved to a warm environment. Conversely, a balloon inflated to capacity in a warm environment will droop if moved to a cool environment. In addition, helium escapes more rapidly from balloons under warm conditions. Barometric pressure can also affect flotation. On days when the barometric pressure is low, some helium-inflated balloons may struggle to float. Elevation can also affect flotation. At high elevations, helium may be unable to support the weight of many types of balloons. Sometimes the choice of balloon ribbon can make a difference in flotation. A shorter, lighter-weight ribbon may help a balloon to float instead of droop at high altitudes.

INFLATION AND SEALING

Whether using air or helium, balloon inflation is a simple process. When properly inflated and sealed, foil balloons typically last three to four weeks or more. The float time for latex balloons is significantly shorter. For example, an average 11-inch latex balloon will last 18 to 24 hours when inflated with helium. Larger latex balloons, which hold more helium, can last 36 hours or more. Templates are useful tools for inflating balloons to the correct size, and balloon "boosters" are products available to help increase the float time of latex balloons. The procedures for using these products and more are outlined in the section that follows.

Air Inflation

Simple, inexpensive hand pumps (Figure 6-1) are available to make inflation of latex balloons, particularly "spaghetti"-type balloons, easier than inflation by mouth. (The most common "spaghetti"-type balloon is a 260, which gets its name from its size when fully inflated—2 inches wide by 60 inches long.) To use a hand pump, slide the neck of the balloon onto the pump nozzle and hold the neck of the balloon in place while sliding the pump up and down, filling the balloon to the desired size. For some balloon projects, such as making balloon animals, it is desirable to control the balloon size by underinflating it. Other projects, particularly party work, warrant the use of an electric air inflator. These machines can be used to inflate both latex and foil balloons with cool air. (Some also can be used for latex or foil balloon deflation, allowing reuse of the balloons.) Foil balloons smaller than 18 inches in diameter will not float when inflated with helium, so these balloons are always inflated with air.

To inflate a balloon with an electric air inflator, slide the neck of the balloon onto the nozzle of the inflator, and hold it in place as you activate the release of air (Figure 6-2). Some machines are operated by foot pedal, others have a valve much like a helium tank, and others operate by a simple flip of a switch. Once the balloon is filled to the desired size, release the valve or foot pedal, or flip the switch to turn the machine off.

Helium Inflation

Most helium tanks have a standard plastic or rubber tip nozzle that is pushed either down or sideways to release the helium (Figure 6-3). The more the nozzle is depressed, the more helium is released. When first learning to inflate balloons, it is best to start slowly. Expect to burst a few balloons. With practice, you will discover your personal comfort level with the speed of inflation.

A number of specialty inflation products are available for those who do a great deal of balloon work. Nozzles are available to inflate multiple balloons at one time or to regulate the amount of helium released into balloons of different types and sizes.

Inflation Size

Most latex balloons are manufactured to be rounded in shape when properly inflated. They should be inflated to the point that they form a full, swollen center and an overall shape much like an inverted teardrop. Latex balloons are overinflated when they become light-bulb or pear shaped (Figure 6-4).

Proper inflation of foil balloons is more difficult to judge. The seams where the two pieces of film bond together can be fragile, so slow and careful inflation is recommended, especially for foil balloons with irregular shapes (stars, flowers, fish, frogs and so on). A fully inflated foil balloon will typically have a taut, drumlike center and a few wrinkles at the edges (Figure 6-5, Page 116). Practice is essential to getting the feel for proper foil balloon inflation. For foolproof results, special inflators are available that automatically inflate foil balloons to the proper pressure.

Figure 6-1. Hand pump for inflating balloons.

Figure 6-2. Electric air inflator.

Figure 6-3. Inflating with a helium tank.

Figure 6-4. Overinflated latex balloon.

Figure 6-5. A properly inflated foil balloon.

Figure 6-6. Cardboard template for balloon sizing.

Figure 6-7. Metal template for balloon sizing.

Templates

Balloons are sold in a wide variety of sizes. In order to get maximum life out of a balloon, it should be inflated to its proper size. Underinflation will do latex balloons no harm, but overinflation can stretch these balloons so that air or helium escapes more readily. Foil balloons do not benefit from underinflation. In fact, an underinflated foil balloon typically will float for little more than a day (versus its potential three- to five-week float time). Overinflation of foil balloons typically causes them to burst.

Balloon templates are available that can help ensure balloons are inflated to their proper sizes. Latex balloon measurements reflect the diameter of a properly inflated balloon. For example, a properly inflated 11-inch balloon will be 11 inches in diameter across the widest portion of the balloon belly. Foil balloon measurements also reflect the measurement of the widest portion of a properly inflated balloon. Templates for standard balloon sizes allow the designer to check the inflation level before sealing. Some templates are simple cardboard cutouts that slide over an inflated balloon (Figure 6-6). Other templates have a pair of metal posts that slide along a measuring stick (Figure 6-7). With this template, a balloon is positioned between the posts to determine the correctness of the inflation level.

Balloon "Boosters"

Several products are available to help make inflated latex balloons last longer. Typically used primarily for helium-inflated balloons, these balloon "boosters" form a barrier on the inside of latex balloons to help reduce the escape of air or helium. In special situations, such as when adding confetti to the exterior of a balloon, balloon booster can be used on the exterior of a balloon as well.

HI-FLOAT® is a widely available balloon booster that comes in several formulations. The use of this product in latex balloons can increase float time up to 25 times that of untreated balloons. In other words, a helium-filled 11-inch balloon that would normally be expected to float 18 to 24 hours has a potential float time of 450-600 hours (or about 19 to 25 days). Thus, the use of balloon booster can extend the life of latex balloons to nearly that of foil balloons.

Place the neck of a latex balloon onto the pump nozzle of a bottle of HI-FLOAT®.

Depress the nozzle until the desired amount of HI-FLOAT® is dispensed. This varies by balloon size. Provided pump adapters regulate the amount.

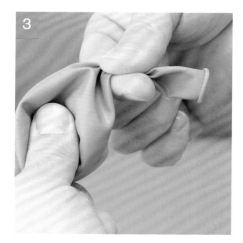

Holding the balloon neck closed, rub the sides of the balloon together to distribute the solution throughout the inside of the balloon. Do not get the solution into the neck.

Inflate the balloon to the proper size. Extension hoses or adapters allow the balloon neck to stay upright. Tie the balloon neck; do not use clips.

Sealing Balloons

Most 18-inch and larger foil balloons on the market today are self-sealing types. These balloons have a valve that seals itself upon removal of the balloon from the inflation nozzle. Self-sealing balloons can be inflated, deflated and re-inflated. They also can be perked up with extra helium, as needed, to extend float time.

To seal a self-sealing foil balloon, simply remove the balloon from the helium nozzle. The valve will close, and helium will be contained within the balloon. To deflate a foil balloon, slide a straw through the neck of the balloon into the belly of the balloon, and press on the balloon to deflate it (Figure 6-8).

Heat Sealing Foil Balloons

For foil balloons that are not self-sealing, a heat sealer is needed for a secure seal. The neck of the balloon should be held between your index and middle fingers, keeping the layers of film flat against one another as opposed to pinched or twisted, then inserted into the sealer (Figure 6-9). Follow the directions on the sealer.

Tying Latex Balloons

Latex balloons are tied most often with a simple knot. Pinch the neck of an inflated latex balloon just beneath the swollen belly. Stretch the neck of the balloon so it extends several inches, and wrap it around your index and middle fingers. Loop the balloon end over the neck, and bring the end through the space between the neck and your fingers (Figure 6-10).

Balloon Fasteners

Other accessories are available from balloon manufacturers to ease the sealing process. Balloon clips allow latex balloons to be sealed with a simple snap. Balloon discs seal latex balloons and attach curling ribbons in one step. When inflating oversized (16-inch or larger) latex balloons or large quantities of balloons, these products can significantly increase speed and decrease finger pain. All accessories add weight, so it is important to be sure the balloon size will hold enough helium to support the extra weight.

Figure 6-8. Deflating a self-sealing foil balloon.

Figure 6-9. Heat-sealing a foil balloon.

Figure 6-10. Tying a latex balloon.

Balloon artists are known to have many tricks that allow balloons to be used in creative and unusual ways. A few simple techniques are provided here to enhance the impact of your balloon bouquets.

Double-Stuffed Balloon

This balloon uses two latex balloons, a clear exterior balloon and a colored interior balloon, to achieve a simple special effect.

DESIGN STEPS

Wrap a 5", 9" or 11" latex balloon around the eraser end of a pencil.

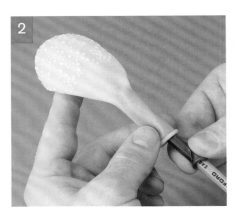

Insert the balloon-covered pencil into the neck of a larger, clear latex balloon.

Holding the necks of both balloons, remove the pencil so the colored balloon remains inside the clear one.

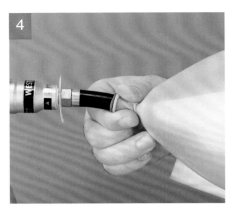

Position the neck of the colored balloon onto a helium tank nozzle. Arrange the neck of the clear balloon over the colored balloon. Inflate the colored balloon to the desired size.

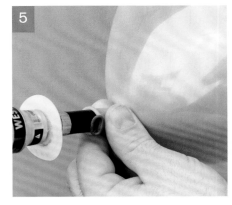

Pinch the necks of the two balloons, and remove them from the nozzle. Then, while still pinching the neck of the colored balloon to maintain inflation, slide the neck of the clear balloon onto the helium tank nozzle.

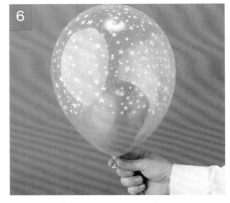

Slowly inflate the clear balloon to its standard size. (Note: The helium will produce a loud noise as it initially squeezes between the layers of latex.) Remove the balloon necks from the nozzle, and knot the two together.

Curly-Q Balloons

These air-inflated balloons make nice accents at the base of helium-inflated latex or foil balloons. Use latex "spaghetti" balloons (either 160's, which are 1 inch by 60 inches when fully inflated or 260's, which are 2 inches by 60 inches when fully inflated).

DESIGN STEPS

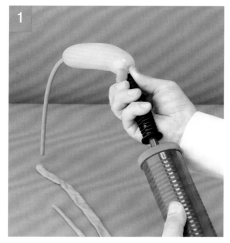

Pre-inflate a spaghetti balloon with an electric or manual air pump. Then deflate the balloon.

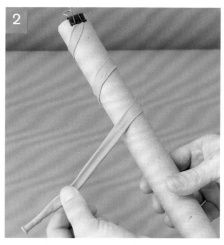

Attach the tip of the balloon to the end of a cardboard roll with a binder clip (rolls from florist foil work well). Wrap the balloon around the cardboard roll.

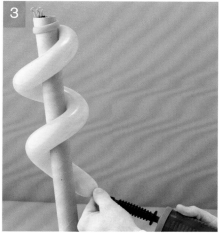

Inflate the balloon while it is still clipped to and wound around the roll with an electric or manual air inflator. Holding the roll between your knees will provide a free hand to maneuver the pump.

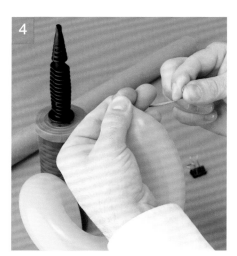

Remove the binder clip to free the balloon from the cardboard roll. Tie a knot in the balloon tail.

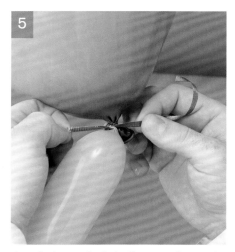

Attach the curly-Q balloon to the neck of a helium-inflated latex or foil balloon with curling ribbon. (Note: A minimum of an 11-inch latex or 18-inch foil balloon is needed to support the added weight of the curly-Q.)

Balloon bouquets are a popular alternative to flower arrangements for special occasions. Only a basic knowledge of balloon design techniques is needed to successfully prepare festive collections of balloons with a multitude of themes and color schemes. Weighting these bouquets is necessary both for proper display and to prevent the balloons from escaping into the environment.

Balloon Bouquet Column

The columnar balloon bouquet is an easy way to assemble a collection of several balloons into a giftlike presentation. It can be designed with as few as four balloons (three in a cluster and one on top) and with balloons of one or many types combined. Consistency among the balloon sizes adds desirable uniformity while an oversized latex or novelty-shaped foil balloon makes a nice topper.

SUGGESTED MATERIALS

7-12 9" helium-inflated latex balloons each with 2 yards of curling ribbon
3 helium-inflated novelty foil balloons
3-4 air-inflated curly-Q balloons
Balloon weights

DESIGN STEPS

Position a trio of balloons so they all rise to the same height.

Create another balloon trio, and add it below so that the tops of the balloons fill the spaces created between the narrow bases of the first trio of balloons.

Choose a balloon to form the top of the bouquet. A novelty-shaped foil balloon provides nice impact. Position this balloon so its base merges with the tops of the three balloons beneath it.

Add two foil balloons at the base of the bouquet.

Attach curly-Q balloons to the necks of three or four balloons within the bouquet with curling ribbon.

Loop the collective ends of curling ribbon, and pull the ends through to create a single knot. Tie the bouquet ribbons to one or more weights.

Domed Variation

While the columnar-shaped bouquet is reasonably easy to deliver, fit through doorways and display in most home and office environments, there are limits to how tall a column can be. When more balloons are desired, the bouquet should become wider, creating a domed shape. Follow these steps to form a domed balloon bouquet.

SUGGESTED MATERIALS

12-15 11" helium-inflated latex balloons
24-30 yards curling ribbon
Balloon weights

DESIGN STEPS

Align multiple balloons of the same type and size into an umbrellalike shape with the balloons side by side. This creates the base of the bouquet.

Thread the ribbons of additional balloons through the canopy, and pull these balloons down from above to "sit" on top of the first balloon layer.

Continue to build the bouquet up and out to incorporate all the balloons. If multiple balloon styles and sizes are included, use the smaller balloons on the top and bottom of the design.

BALLOON ACCESSORIES

Decorative weights are available to anchor helium balloons (Figure 6-11). And for adding balloons to arrangements, saucers and straws (also referred to as cups and sticks), can be used (Figure 6-12).

To create decorative holders to secure air-inflated balloons within arrangements, flexible wire stems can be attached to balloons as shown here.

Figure 6-11. Balloon weights.

Figure 6-12. Balloon saucer and straw.

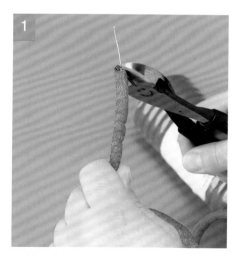

Pull back the foam, uncovering ½" of the wire inside, and clip the wire off so it won't come in contact with the balloon.

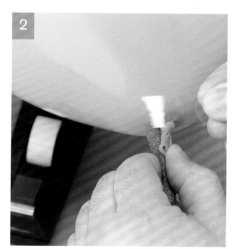

Tape the knotted stem of a latex balloon to the wireless end of the flexible foam stem. Curl or shape the wire to create a decorative effect. Trim the stem to the length needed, and insert it into a vase or floral foam like a flower stem.

VII

DISPLAYS

The ability to showcase floral designs together with other related products in a manner that makes the merchandise look attractive and appealing is an important skill for any floral designer. Whether displays are in a window or inside a store, visual merchandising requires the use of a variety of elements and principles in order to achieve a desirable outcome.

elements in harmony

To some degree, designing attractive displays is much like designing attractive floral arrangements. Great color and an eye-catching focal point are highly desirable but may not be enough to make a display (or arrangement) click. Multiple components must be considered and controlled in order to achieve success.

FLORAL DISPLAY TYPES

Most floral shops utilize a combination of window displays and interior displays that include both **decorative displays** and **functional displays**. Decorative displays (Figure 7-1), which involve the artistic placement of merchandise and accompanying props, tend to dominate flower shops. Functional displays (Figure 7-2), which feature masses or rows of products presented with little or no special arrangement (think cereal boxes, battery displays and so on), are minimal.

A **vignette** (Figure 7-3) is a type of decorative display designed to mimic a small, familiar setting or view. Often these displays attempt to capture the feeling of a moment in time, such as a romantic table for two, a bride's dressing quarters or a patio garden. Vignettes are especially popular means of presenting floral merchandise and offer the advantage of showing products in a setting representing their intended use. The disadvantage of these displays is the tremendous maintenance required because well-designed decorative displays move merchandise rapidly.

DISPLAY ELEMENTS

The elements of any display are the components used to put it together. Merchandise and props are the key physical components to any display. Other components, such as backgrounds and signage, are the subtle elements that influence the visual impact and sales appeal of a display. An understanding of these elements and how each contributes to an effective display is important to the process of successful visual merchandising.

Theme

Many displays, particularly window displays, are centered around a chosen theme. There are a variety of themes that make effective floral displays.

Seasonal themes reflect the look, mood or feeling of winter, spring, summer or fall (Figure 7-4 on Page 124). Such displays often depict a familiar scene and may reflect the traditional colors and symbols of each season (e.g., pastels for spring with kites and butterflies or warm hues for autumn with falling leaves and sheaves of wheat) or maybe a more creative interpretation (e.g., a spring night sky or an autumn campfire).

Figure 7-1. Decorative display.

Figure 7-2. Functional display.

Figure 7-3. Vignette display.

Figure 7-4. Autumn theme display.

Figure 7-5. Valentine's Day display.

Figure 7-6. Wedding display.

Figure 7-7. County fair display.

Theme *continued*

When using seasonal themes for displays, timing is important. Most often, these displays have the greatest impact when presented during the weeks prior to the season. In other words, an autumn display is more effective in late August and early September than it is in October or November.

Holiday themes are common choices in flower shops where business routinely cycles from one holiday to the next. Major holidays for floral displays are Valentine's Day (Figure 7-5), Easter, Mother's Day, Thanksgiving and Christmas. Additional important holidays that are sometimes incorporated into the display plan include St. Patrick's Day, Administrative Professionals Week, Memorial Day, Father's Day, Independence Day, Halloween, Hanukkah and Kwanzaa. Some holidays, such as Sweetest Day, are important regionally but not nationally. Other "holidays," such as Groundhog Day, May Day, National Rose Month (June) and Grandparents Day, have the potential for development through strong promotions including displays.

Life events such as birthdays, anniversaries, weddings (Figure 7-6) and graduations make good themes for floral displays because flowers are often a part of these celebrations. Any event that represents a life stage or transition—engagement, new baby, prom and so on—is a theme worth considering.

Timing is important for many life-event-themed displays because the goal is to capture the attention of shoppers at the time floral purchases for such life events are on their mind. While birthdays take place throughout the year, graduations and proms are primarily spring events. Displays promoting flowers for these occasions would best be in place between April and June. Although many weddings take place during this same spring time period, the best times to promote wedding flowers are the months following occasions when many engagements occur, such as January (for Christmas engagements) and March (for Valentine's Day engagements).

Community events held throughout the year provide opportunities for a business to tie window displays with local events and activities. A community daddy-daughter dance or 5K race can provide a useful display theme with signage that suggests customers "Get Your Girls Corsages for the Dance" or "Dash in for Flowers." A local jazz festival, community craft show, Oktoberfest or county fair (Figure 7-7) are all events that could be supported through shop displays that simultaneously promote floral products.

"Back to School" is a universal theme that all communities experience in late summer. Displays that showcase plants and flowers on desktops, that are designed in apple-themed containers, or that create a nostalgic schoolhouse setting with floral adornments are appropriate for this community event theme.

Educational displays take a different approach than many of the scenery-oriented themes. Displays utilizing an educational theme attempt to provide information and dispense knowledge to potential clients (Figure 7-8). These displays can be effective by sharing business or product-related information of which the average shopper might be unaware. For example, an educational display that showcases a wide array of flower types, each labeled with the scientific name and country of origin, helps customers better understand the products you offer and helps them appreciate the world-wide sources from which your flowers arrive.

Promotional displays draw their themes from offers for a single product or a select group of products. These displays are less about creating a thematic setting than they are about communicating a new merchandise line, a sale or a special limited-time offer. Promotional displays are especially effective when tied to advertising and promotional campaigns broadcast to a wide audience. A store window filled with new permanent flowers displayed like a luxurious garden, or an in-store display of baskets stacked or suspended in a creative configuration, are displays that effectively promote a single product line without the need for complicated construction (Figure 7-9).

Attention-Grabbers

Good visual merchandising typically incorporates one or more elements that attract the eyes and hold attention long enough to inspire customers' interest in the products displayed. Attention-grabbers come in many forms.

Color, particularly bold colors or strong contrasting colors, is an excellent tool for attracting attention to displays. Warm colors (reds, oranges and yellows) are more effective from a distance than cool colors (green, blue and violet). Monochromatic displays (Figure 7-10) that utilize tints, tones and shades of a single hue have greater impact than polychromatic displays that combine many or all colors. Even cool colors, which tend to recede into the background of most color combinations, hold their own when used in a monochromatic display.

Motion is also an automatic attention-getter. When objects in a display exhibit movement, attention is quickly pulled away from stationary objects to whatever is moving. Mechanical figures, motorized turntables, fans that blow suspended objects and blinking lights are all effective means of creating motion and attracting attention.

Implied motion also can be used as an attention-grabber. Props or merchandise items are assembled in a way that implies something is happening even though nothing is physically moving (Figure 7-11). A rascally rabbit may appear to bound over a fence in search of treats, or a faux waterfall of blue wired ribbon cascading in arched layers may mimic falling water. Actual and implied motion can be combined within a single display, but the display artist must exercise restraint because too many forms of motion in one display can make it too busy for viewers to maintain focus.

Size, most often in the form of oversized objects, is another potential means of attracting attention. While it is always important to consider scale and proportion in any display (to be sure objects are appropriately sized to the display space and to each other), some displays seek to attract attention by utilizing one or many items that are intentionally out of proportion. A single sunflower blossom that spans the width of a window or a sunflower stem that appears to grow through the ceiling is oversized to the point that it attracts attention (Figure 7-12).

Figure 7-8. Educational display.

Figure 7-9. Promotional display.

Figure 7-12. Oversized-object display.

Figure 7-10. Monochromatic display.

Figure 7-11. Display with implied motion.

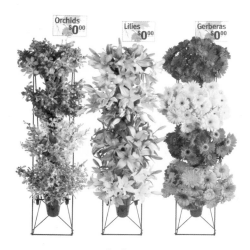

Figure 7-13. Shadowbox effect in an undersized display.

Figure 7-14. Mass display.

Attention-Grabbers *continued*

Under the right circumstances, **undersizing** also can be an effective attention-getter. The display must be positioned in an area with significant foot traffic since the small items on display will require viewing from close proximity. A large window display or display case can be converted to draw attention to miniature flowers or tiny giftware items by blacking out the bulk of the display space with paper, Mylar or foil. An opening can be left in the window cover in a size proportionate to the item(s) on display, creating an intriguing shadowbox effect (Figure 7-13).

Humor and **surprise** are fun methods of attracting attention to displays. Silly signage, playful themes and unconventional presentations of familiar items are ways to draw viewers. To use humor effectively, displays needn't be hilarious, just humorous enough to cause a chuckle or a smile. Cupid shooting roses instead of arrows or the Easter bunny with his feet stuck in the mud are simple images that defy convention.

Flower shops that prefer to maintain a highbrow image may not be comfortable with the idea of creating humorous displays. Used sparingly, however, and with a measure of good taste, humor and surprise can fit into nearly any setting. For example, a display of elegant vases holding collections of marbles, candies, straws, cutlery, socks, mail and so on, paired with a sign that states "Flowers Optional," demonstrates a sense of humor without being over the top.

The use of **mass** and **repetition** are two additional means of attracting attention to displays. Just as an enormous tower of stacked grapefruits captures the attention of shoppers in the produce section of the supermarket, masses of a single product or groups of related products become attention-getters among floral merchandise (Figure 7-14). Two or three plush monkeys displayed throughout the flower shop get lost in the merchandise mix; however, a display of many monkeys in baskets or barrels gains impact based on mass. In the supermarket, the stacked grapefruits capture greater attention when oranges and apples are stacked as well. In the floral shop, the monkey display gains strength when plush animal friends are displayed to form an entire "jungle" of wildlife suspended on a repeated series of ropes and vines.

Merchandise

Merchandise is an important element in any type of display. It is the primary element in in-store displays but may sometimes be a secondary element in window displays that seek to depict a chosen theme with extensive props and accessories. As much as possible, it is imperative that merchandise be presented front and center, in a manner that encourages customer interaction. Window displays should present merchandise in a manner that inspires customers to enter the shop for a closer look.

Merchandise in window displays may or may not have prices visible. Retailers often debate the merits of showing prices in window displays. Some believe that by not showing prices, customer traffic increases due to customers who must enter the shop for price information. Others believe that potential customers are lost when customers see merchandise without tags and assume the price is beyond their means, thus never entering the store to find out the price. A good rule of thumb regarding the pricing of window merchandise is to be consistent. If one item is displayed with a visible price, then all of the merchandise should be visibly priced.

Props and Fixtures

Good displays require fixtures on which to attractively place the merchandise, and props to enhance the setting. Many **standard store fixtures** are available to provide

Figure 7-15. Potential props.

floor, tabletop, wall and ceiling display options. Some of the best display fixtures for floral products tend to be **unique** or **one-of-a-kind units** that run the gamut from antique armoires to art-deco tables, from earthy wooden pedestals to glass- or marble-topped counters. Fixtures such as these contribute greatly not only to the effective display of floral products but also to creating a sense of style and personality for the business.

Display props come in many forms. Some are decorative, such as faux pastries or paper parasols; others are mechanical, such as risers or fabric remnants. Theme displays often call for special props that must be constructed or can be purchased or rented from prop shops or other sources. Versatile props that offer the potential for use in multiple displays are a worthwhile investment (Figure 7-15).

Foam-centered board is frequently used to create display props. This three-ply board, made with an inner core of plastic foam sandwiched between two sheets of poster board, is both lightweight and easy to cut with a utility knife. Using an overhead projector, images can be projected onto the board, traced and cut out to provide unlimited prop options (Figure 7-16). Corsage pins can be used to assemble multiple pieces of foam board into three-dimensional props as well.

Figure 7-16. Tulips from foam-centered board.

While props are key to visual merchandising, avoid overwhelming a display with too many props at the expense of the merchandise and intended display message.

Backgrounds

Backgrounds are important to help maintain the focus on the merchandise displayed. When one display bleeds into another without any delineation between them, it is difficult for each individual display to hold its own, the sales messages become confused and customers lose interest.

Modern window displays often have **open backgrounds** rather than **closed backgrounds**. While this is desirable for attracting customers—a busy shop with high customer traffic will attract curious passers-by who want to find out what's happening inside—it creates the need for **partial visual barriers** so the visibility of the display is maximized. Background materials for shop or window use include:

Figure 7-17. Fabric background.

- **Fabric** - Hang fabric in narrow panels (Figure 7-17) or in a crisscross pattern of strips. For a different look, allow some visibility between fabric pieces rather than aligning one directly beside another.

- **Foam-centered board** - Suspend white or colored panels at varied heights to create geometric patterns, or use one to three panels behind key focal areas (Figure 7-18).

- **Plywood** - Create the look of wainscoting with a half wall of plywood topped with decorative molding.

- **Lattice** - Create a floor-to-ceiling lattice wall to back an open window display or divide a single open display space into two. Cut diamond-shaped windows intermittently along the wall to open the views beyond.

- **Ribbon** - Hang strips of varied types, widths and colors of ribbon in various lengths to form a continuous curtain or light screen (Figure 7-19 on Page 128).

- **Curtains** - Purchase curtains or make your own, using the fabric panels draped and gathered to one or both sides of a window or interior display space.

Figure 7-18. Foam-centered board background.

Figure 7-19. Ribbon background.

Figure 7-20. Fall display with signs.

Figure 7-21. Display with varied levels.

Backgrounds *continued*

- **Cellophane** or **foil** - Use these or any lightweight film to create horizontal or vertical stripes or a patchwork design. Or roll pieces into strips and twist them together to form decorative ropes. Crumple, then unfold the pieces for a textured effect.

- **Plants** - Use risers to elevate plants to varied levels and form a natural green screen, or place plants of varied sizes across the display floor for a similar effect. Cover the plant pots with dark fabric or moss.

- **Branches** - Insert a series of birch branches into a base of moss-covered plastic foam to form either a light or a dense screen.

Signs

Not all displays require signs, but many benefit from them. Signs in the windows and display areas of the shop serve as **silent salespeople**, constantly providing messages about what customers are viewing and, either directly or indirectly, encouraging sales (Figure 7-20).

Use signs in displays to help communicate the themes. Sometimes a display message may be clear to no one other than the display artist until a sign explains the concept. Use signs to announce prices, especially when a sale or special promotion is offered. Use signs to describe merchandise features and benefits (e.g., the long vase life of *Alstroemerias*). Use signs also to provide information that would be interesting to customers and increase sales appeal. For instance, if a crystal vase is from the "Preston Bailey" collection, mentioning Mr. Bailey's industry acclaim and celebrity clientele could arouse greater interest in the product.

Signs should always be **brief** and **direct**, with wording that is not only concise but also clever and catchy. Messages should sound professional and look professional as well. Computer-generated signs are preferable to hand-written ones unless the handwriting is stylish, highly readable and consistently used throughout the shop. Even computer-generated signs can be inferior if the combination of type sizes and styles, ink colors and paper types is poorly planned. For these reasons, it is often a good idea to work with a graphic artist to establish a consistent style for all shop signage.

DISPLAY PRINCIPLES

The process of assembling display elements into an attractive and appealing display requires the use of many artistic principles. While experience is the best teacher, the explanations of the principles that follow will help guide the display process.

Viewpoint

Displays should be designed from the perspective of the viewers. Window displays that are seen from a distance require large props that make a quick statement as vehicular traffic passes by. Foot traffic in front of a window requires smaller-scale displays with more detail.

In-store displays should make the most of the full complement of display space from floor to ceiling. Varied levels within a display ensure that something is at eye level for viewers of all ages and heights (Figure 7-21).

Broad display spaces, especially windows, should be designed by keeping in mind the way they will likely be "read" (e.g., left to right, top to bottom) by the viewers. Whenever possible, these spaces should incorporate an attention-grabber near the upper left portion of the display and a focal element in the bottom right (Figure 7-22).

Focal Point

Flower arrangements typically are designed with a central **focal point**, and displays should be, too. A focal point can be created using a single large element or a mass of smaller elements in one area of the display. This focal area should clearly dominate the other portions of the display (Figure 7-23).

The focal point is often positioned in the center of a display, but it may be placed anywhere as long as it is balanced by components in the remainder of the display space. Multiple focal areas also may be used across a horizontal display (Figure 7-24) or up and down a vertical display; however, one focal area should clearly dominate a bit more than the rest.

Figure 7-22. Display with attention-grabber near top left and focal element at bottom right.

Figure 7-23. Ivy-covered bunny as dominant focal point.

Figure 7-24. Multiple focal areas in a horizontal display.

Scale and Proportion

The size relationships of the display to the display space (**scale**) and of the display elements to each other (**proportion**) are important to the cohesiveness of a display. The size and amount of material placed within a display must reasonably fill the space without leaving it too vacant or too crowded. In order to achieve good scale, a large window display needs large props and ample merchandise. These elements would seem out of scale in a small window display space. The same concept is true within the shop (Figure 7-25).

Figure 7-25. Scale and proportion.

Figure 7-26. Symmetrically balanced display.

Figure 7-27. Asymmetrically balanced display.

Figure 7-28. Spacing emphasizes a focal area.

Scale and Proportion *continued*

Proportion is an issue when combining display props, fixtures and merchandise. Similar size and quantity issues apply. For instance, a trio of pillar candles grouped together on a tabletop pedestal represents a better sense of proportion than a single pillar candle alone. The same candle trio on a floor-standing pedestal has a proportion problem due to the added pedestal height.

Balance

The visual weight contributed by the elements in a display must be balanced in order for the display to be comfortable on the eyes. A display may be balanced either symmetrically or asymmetrically. **Symmetrically balanced displays** are the easiest to design. In these displays, whatever items are positioned on one side of the display are repeated on the other side with matching items. Often, symmetrical displays have a single, centered focal area (Figure 7-26).

Asymmetrical balance requires a bit more effort than symmetrical, but the results frequently provide a greater sense of style and flair. An **asymmetrically balanced display**, when visually divided down the center, has a different combination of display element sizes and quantities on each side. Despite these differences, the total visual weight contributed by these objects is equivalent (Figure 7-27). For example, three square pedestals in a stair-stepped arrangement on the left side of a display might be counter-balanced by a single round table on the right. To continue the asymmetrical balance, a moderate-sized vase arrangement and two large vases might fill the three pedestals while a large mass design anchors the table.

Space and Order

Organization of the display components within the window or in-store display space is essential to a successful display. When props and merchandise are scattered with seemingly no relationship, they quickly lose impact. **Space** must be designed within a display much like it is in an arrangement. In the focal area of the display, elements may be somewhat concentrated without a great deal of space between them. This helps give the focal area the desired level of dominance. Items farther from the focal area may have greater space between them but not so much that they feel disconnected from the whole (Figure 7-28).

Important points to remember when considering the space and order of a display are:

- **Avoid clutter.** Too much merchandise, no matter how well arranged, tends to look messy and confused.

- **Don't try to show everything at once.** Edit the choices of merchandise to be featured in decorative displays, and relegate the remaining product to routine presentation on display shelves. Also, avoid overwhelming merchandise by surrounding it with too many display props.

- **Maintain a relationship among display components.** The greater the quantity of merchandise included, the more it needs to be related in a clear way, be it color, style, use or other notable relationship.

Figure 7-29. Stair-stepped rhythm.

Figure 7-30. Zigzag lines creating rhythm.

Rhythm

Rhythm in displays provides a visual pathway for the eyes to follow. Ideally, that pathway leads to the focal point of the display and may be so effective that it entertains the eyes back and forth several times along the same pathway. Visual rhythm can be created in a number of ways. Some of the most common uses of rhythm involve **stair-stepped elements** (stepping either up, down or both) (Figure 7-29), **zigzag lines** (formed by a background of sticks, fabric strips or objects such as parasols) (Figure 7-30) and **radial placements** (with small elements placed about a focal point like rays of the sun).

Harmony and Unity

Harmony is an important principle when creating displays because it ensures that the elements have a notable relationship that provides a pleasing finished product. Sometimes the relationship is based on color, such as a Valentine's Day window filled with merchandise and props that are red. Other times the relationship among items is formed by the display theme, such as summer gardening gadgets or birthday party décor. When the display components look right together, the harmony is successful (Figure 7-31).

Unity refers to the success of all the display components to create a finished composition that has a feeling of oneness. Despite the inherent space between objects, a well-unified display looks connected and complete. When all the other principles are successfully applied, unity usually follows quite naturally.

Figure 7-31. Harmony in forms, materials and colors.

Creating a few exciting displays takes thought and effort. Creating a full year of dynamic displays in windows and inside the store requires not only inspiration and perspiration but also substantial planning. To develop an annual plan, follow the steps outlined here.

1 **Get a calendar.** Start with a new calendar with big blank boxes. Write in all the important floral holidays for the coming year as well as any major community events for which you expect to devote display space. Investigate potential minor holidays around which you could build floral sales (such as Groundhog Day in February or National Rose Month in June). Consider also whether there are significant religious or ethnic populations in your community that might be reached by promotion of holidays such as *Cinco de Mayo*.

2 **Schedule the major displays.** Plot out the days and weeks prior to each holiday that displays should be in place. Generally, the more important the holiday is to total shop revenue, the more time and space should be devoted to it. A three- to five-week span is reasonable for most displays. Use holiday-colored markers to show the days that will be devoted to each display. For holidays that fall close to one another on the calendar, which is sometimes the case with Easter and Administrative Professionals Week (the last full week of April) or with Sweetest Day and National Bosses Day (both in mid-October), choose one to promote with a window display and use an in-store display to promote the other.

3 **Fill the gaps.** Once the calendar is marked with the holiday display schedule, begin to fill the gaps between display periods with displays that relate to seasons, life events and community events. Seasonal displays are most effective when presented shortly before or early within the season at hand. A winter scene is not particularly desirable once temperatures plummet, just as a summer scene is not a desirable reminder of scalding August heat.

Life events, such as birthdays, anniversaries and new babies, occur year-round and thus, displays based on these events can be scheduled at nearly any time. Some life or community events, such as proms and graduations, dictate the most appropriate display timing, while others, such as weddings, require careful consideration of not only when the event may fall but also when customers' flower planning takes place. For instance, a wedding display in January appeals to potential brides who became engaged at Christmas.

4 **Educate and promote.** Seek opportunities between planned displays to educate customers with simple displays that show where your flowers come from around the world, what their botanical names are and so on. Choose specific product lines (vases, baskets, potted plants, etc.) to promote one at a time throughout the year during the limited days between one major display and the next. When possible, choose promotions to tie in with special promotions offered by product manufacturers.

5 **Select themes.** Once the calendar is filled, return to the major displays and select a theme for each that will provide a direction for future planning. Holiday themes that are original and clever will stand a better chance of gaining customer attention in a retail marketplace filled with the predictable holiday symbols. So cast aside all plans for conventional cupids, bunnies and Santa in favor of displays that offer unique interpretations of each holiday theme and color scheme. Ask yourself "What will other retailers do?" and then plan to do something else.

6 **Put it on paper.** Develop each display plan in the months before assembly, including a rough sketch and a list of necessary props, both those on hand and others that will need to be purchased or constructed. Determine what the attention-grabber will be for each display. The bold use of color, a humorous message, elements in motion, oversized objects and masses of flowers are all effective means of attracting attention. Become a scout for suitable display props and accessories that fit your plans. The best finds are often discovered when you are least expecting them, but with a plan in mind, you will always be on the lookout.

7 **Assign a leader.** List a leader for each display on the completed calendar. Assigning responsibility ensures that one person will be central to the planning and construction process. This individual can funnel ideas from staff, gather props, order merchandise, create signage and lead the display setup to ensure that important design principles, including proportion, scale, balance and focal point, are properly applied to the finished display. In addition, this individual should monitor the display plan to ensure that it remains focused on flowers or floral-related products. Finally, the display leader should ensure that the display is removed in a timely manner so that Santa isn't still hanging around when Cupid arrives.

DISPLAY CHECKLIST

There is much to keep in mind while assembling a display. Use this checklist to guide the display process or to evaluate the results.

❏ Use themes to give window and decorative in-store displays a sense of personality and purpose.

❏ Time seasonal displays before, rather than during, the season depicted.

❏ Use promotional displays to reinforce advertising of special sales and store events.

❏ Incorporate one or more attention-grabbing elements, including color, motion, size, humor or surprise, into every display.

❏ In displays that use numerous props and fixtures, make sure the merchandise you are selling dominates.

❏ Price all merchandise within in-store displays. Be consistent in pricing (or not pricing) merchandise in window displays.

❏ Invest in versatile display props that offer the potential for use in displays throughout the year.

❏ Use backgrounds to separate in-store displays from one another.

❏ Maintain visibility through window display backgrounds into the shop to attract greater customer traffic.

❏ Use professional-looking signs to communicate display themes, announce prices and special promotions, and provide product information.

❏ Design displays from the viewpoint of the viewers, with a left-to-right, top-to-bottom arrangement that matches the habit of reading left to right.

❏ Vary the levels of merchandise within displays so there is something at eye level for customers of all ages and heights.

❏ Establish a central focal point within each display and balance it, either symmetrically or asymmetrically, with supporting display components on each side.

❏ Avoid cluttering displays with elements that are not essential to the big picture. Maintain breathing space between focal elements and other display components.

❏ Create a rhythmic visual pathway that leads the eye from an attention-grabbing element to the focal point.

❏ Locate functional displays (with merchandise massed in baskets, rows and stacks) near the decorative displays that showcase the same products in use.

❏ Mix warm-colored and cool-colored displays throughout the store to help pull customers from one display setting to the next.

❏ Refresh decorative displays daily because these displays encourage constant customer interaction.

VIII

PACKAGING

Flowers require special packaging. To ensure safe travel from the flower shop to their final destination, flowers must be wrapped in a manner that protects them from the weather as well as rough handling. Arrangements must be padded and stabilized so they will stay upright. Corsages and boutonnieres fare best when boxed or bagged while plants benefit from paper or plastic sleeves. Gift baskets, an extension of traditional floral giftware lines, provide special packaging challenges of their own.

Not every bloom sold in flower shops needs to be wrapped. Sometimes customers prefer the simplicity of presenting an unwrapped blossom or bouquet. However, when wrapping is called for, it should be not only functional but also decorative.

TO WRAP OR NOT TO WRAP

The decision to wrap or not to wrap a flower presentation often depends on customer preferences. For arrangements, the container in which the flowers are designed also influences this choice. Upright vases, footed bowls and round dishes all have a tendency to tip or roll. These designs usually need a supportive delivery base or box to help them travel even short distances.

Typically, the primary factor that determines the need to wrap is the weather. When weather conditions are ideal, flowers do not require wrappings. Under less-than-ideal circumstances, packaging is a must.

WEATHER CONDITIONS

Weather conditions of many kinds influence the packaging of floral products. Typically, floral wrappings are considered mandatory in cold weather; however, this is not always the case. In fact, there are as many warm weather conditions that warrant special packaging as there are cold conditions.

Most fresh flowers tolerate cool conditions well. Tropical flowers, which prefer storage temperatures between 45 F and 60 F, are the exception. Arrangements and bouquets of nontropical flowers can be safely stored at temperatures as low as 33 F. When the temperature is above this level, wrapping is not a necessity.

Warm weather also warrants floral packaging, particularly when the temperature is above 90 F. A light wrap of paper or tissue protects flowers from direct sunlight. On warm, windy days, such wrappings also help maintain high relative humidity, which reduces transpiration, helping to keep the flowers turgid (firm and full of water). Wrappings placed around precooled flowers (flowers that have been in refrigeration after design and before sale or delivery) also help extend the benefits of the cooler environment.

Wind is an important weather condition to consider in cold conditions as well. On cold days when the temperature appears to be safe for flowers (above 33 F), moderate winds can create enough of a chill to cause damage, so wrapping becomes necessary. When temperatures and/or wind chills dip significantly below freezing, double wrapping is required to preserve flower life.

Rain, sleet and hail are additional weather conditions that factor into the decision to wrap or not wrap. Any of these conditions are cause for wrapping flowers in order to protect them from these potentially damaging forces of nature.

WRAPPING LOOSE STEMS AND BOUQUETS

Fresh flowers can be wrapped using a variety of packaging products. Paper and tissue provide a traditional-looking wrap while cellophane dresses up the flowers. Standard wrapping methods for loose stems and tied bouquets are provided here, with variations for different wraps or finishing details.

Rolled Rose Wrap

Roses are frequently sold singly as token gifts or to make simple romantic statements. Buried deep within heavy paper wraps, they lose their impact and appeal. This simple wrapping procedure presents the rose inside a window of rolled cellophane. The technique may be used with other flowers as long as they are not too large or widely branched.

SUGGESTED MATERIALS
Single rose (or other similarly sized flower)
Clear cellophane, approximately 8″ wide x 24″-30″ long
Hand stapler or cellophane tape
½ yard ribbon

PACKAGING STEPS

Lay the rose along the long edge of the wrap with the rose head about 2″ - 3″ from the top.

Roll the wrap with the rose inside to form a tube around the flower. Secure the edge of the wrap with tape or staples.

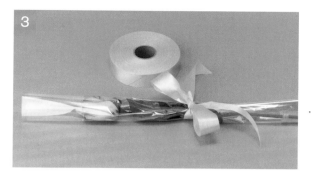

Using about ½ yard of ribbon, tie a bow around the midsection of the package, making sure the ribbon is tight enough to hold the rose in its position inside the package.

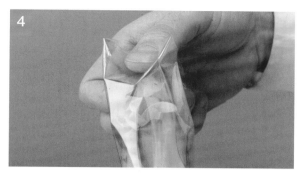

Square the wrap at the top of the tube above the rose head, and create a fold as you would when wrapping the end of a gift box. Trim the rose stem, if desired, so it is no longer than the wrap.

Secure the fold with tape.

(Note: Some customers desire the maximum stem length possible. Also, it may be desirable to store wrapped roses in a vase of water. Under either of these circumstances, the flower stem should be left intact outside the package.)

Rolled Rose Wrap Variation

I. Top-Tied Package

For a festive alternative look, lay the rose along the edge of the wrap, with the rose head about 5 inches to 6 inches from the top. Wrap as directed in Step 2. Tie the package at the midsection and again at the top with multiple pieces of curling ribbon, gathering the wrap comfortably above the flower. Curl the ribbons by sliding each piece along the back of a knife or ribbon shear (Figure 8-1).

Figure 8-1. Top-tied package, a variation on the rolled rose wrap.

Wrapped Stems or Bouquets

Cash-and-carry flowers, such as a handful of tulips, one dozen roses or a mixed collection of garden blooms, typically are wrapped in paper or tissue, or both. Single blooms also can be wrapped the same way using slightly less paper and fewer supportive greens. The standard floral industry wrapping procedure for a bouquet of several flowers is described here, followed by several practical variations.

SUGGESTED MATERIALS

Floral wrapping paper, about 30" x 36"
1-2 sheets waxed tissue paper
Multiple flower stems or mixed bouquet
  with accompanying foliage such as
  leatherleaf fern
Consumer flower-food packet(s)
Hand stapler
Fresh flower care tag

PACKAGING STEPS

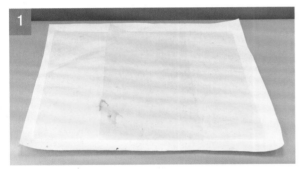

Lay the floral wrapping paper on a flat surface. Position the waxed tissue (waxed side up) on top of the floral wrap. Fold or cut the tissue, if needed, to fit within the wrapping paper.

Lay a bed of three to five stems of foliage on the tissue, with tips angled toward the upper left corner. (For ready-made mixed bouquets with stems tied or otherwise bound, skip this step.)

Lay several flower stems on top of the foliage at the same angle, following a stair-stepped pattern that forms a triangular outline. Place smaller flowers at the top, and reserve larger and/or more special flowers for the focal area at the base.
(For ready-made bouquets, lay the entire bouquet on the waxed tissue at the prescribed angle.)

Add filler flowers, as desired, throughout the process of positioning the stair-stepped flower placements. Finish by placing two or three additional pieces of foliage to cover and soften the appearance of the flower stems.

Trim the stem ends, if needed, so they are equal in length and shorter than the length of the paper.

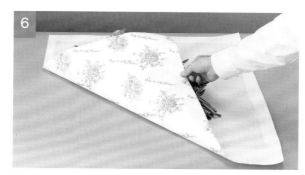

Fold the bottom left corner of the floral wrap across the midsection of the flowers.

Fold the bottom right corner of the wrap up toward the top left corner to cover the stem ends.

Holding the paper in the folded positions, roll the flowers toward the top right corner.

With the rolled package back to its original position, staple the paper along one side to secure the wrap.

Staple the fresh flower care tag and flower-food packet(s) to the exterior of the package.

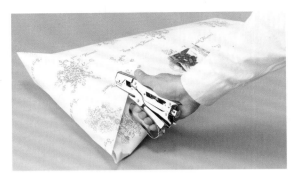

Figure 8-2. Cold weather coverage.

Figure 8-3. Cellophane window wrap.

Figure 8-4. Decorative belt.

Wrapped Stems or Bouquets Variations

I. Cold Weather Coverage

To cover and protect the flowers, close the top of the package by folding the top corner of the wrap over the flowers, stapling to secure it (Figure 8-2).

II. Cellophane Window Wrap

For a more decorative package with visible flowers, use clear cellophane instead of paper wrap. Eliminate the waxed tissue, or pouf the tissue (by pinching it in the center and fluffing it so all the corners flow in the same direction) and place it behind the flowers (Figure 8-3).

III. Decorative Belt

To hold the flowers in place and add a decorative flair, tie a ribbon around the wrapped package and cinch it tight enough to create a "waistline" across the middle of the package (Figure 8-4).

IV. Bouquet Sleeves

Ready-made bouquet sleeves are manufactured in shapes and sizes that accommodate standard floral bouquets. To place a ready-made (hand-tied) bouquet into a bouquet sleeve, fluff the sleeve open, then slide the stems in from the top opening until they emerge through the lower, narrow opening. Bind the sleeve around the stems with a twist tie or, for a more decorative touch, ribbon or raffia (Figure 8-5).

For a loose collection of flowers, gather the blooms to a common height. Surround the flowers with a few pieces of foliage. Trim the stems so they are all the same length, and bind them with a twist-tie. Sleeve the flowers as described above for ready-made bouquets (Figure 8-6).

Some cellophane sleeves are made with a sealed bottom end. For these sleeves, the bound flowers are dropped in from the top, and the top of the sleeve is folded and stapled (Figure 8-7).

Figure 8-5. Ready-made bouquet in sleeve.

Figure 8-6. Loose flowers in sleeve.

Figure 8-7. Flowers in sealed-bottom sleeve.

PACKAGING LOOSE FLOWERS IN BOXES

Roses are commonly packaged in boxes for ease of carriage as well as special presentation. Other flowers can be boxed as well. The steps provided here are for roses but can be modified easily for other flower combinations.

Cardboard rose boxes are commonly available in 24-inch, 30-inch and 36-inch lengths. When rose stems exceed the length of the box, and the customer prefers to maintain the stem length, a box with a perforated end flap can accommodate the extra length. Clear plastic rose boxes, including single-rose boxes, provide an alternative to cardboard. When these boxes are used, the tissue paper lining can be eliminated to provide a clear view of the flowers.

SUGGESTED MATERIALS

Standard florist rose box
1-2 sheets waxed tissue
12 roses
8-10 stems leatherleaf fern
5-7 stems filler, such as tree fern,
  plumosa fern and/or baby's breath

12 water tubes
Consumer flower-food packet(s)
Fresh flower or rose care tag
1-1½ yards #9-width ribbon

PACKAGING STEPS

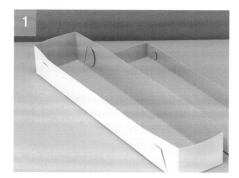

Fold and assemble the rose box and lid.

Pleat one or two sheets of waxed tissue to fit the interior of the box.

Fill 12 water tubes with flower-food solution, and place them on the ends of the rose stems.

Lay two pieces of leatherleaf fern into the flower box, with tips near one end.

Lay a row of four roses side by side on top of the foliage, with the flower heads about 2" from the top of the box.

Add one or two pieces of leatherleaf fern and/or one or two pieces of filler flowers on top of the roses, with tips just beneath the flower heads.

Position a second row of roses atop the greens and filler, leaving about 1" between the bases of the upper roses and the tops of the lower roses for overhang.

Repeat Steps 6-7, forming a third row of roses.

Position three or four stems of leather-leaf fern in the opposite direction, covering the rose stems. Slide the leather-leaf stems under the flowers so only the decorative portion of the greenery is visible.

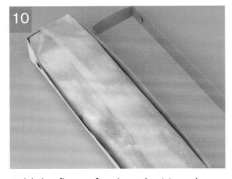

Add the flower-food packet(s) and care tag at the stem end of the box; then fold the tissue over the flowers.

Place the lid on the flower box, and tie a ribbon around the box toward the end that contains the flower heads. (This will help the carrier recognize which end should be held upright.)

Packaging Loose Flowers in Boxes Variation

I. Double-Ended Flower Presentation

A popular variation for boxed roses presents the flower heads in both ends of the box. To do so, follow Steps 1-4 (Page 141) in one end of the box, and repeat the steps in the opposite end of the box. Then, lay a row of three roses, with heads side by side, on top of the foliage, about 2 inches from the top of the box. Repeat the rose placements on the opposite end of the box. Follow Steps 6-7 (Pages 141 and 142) at each end of the box, using three roses in each row instead of four. Lay stems of leatherleaf fern on top of the rose stems in each direction to cover them. Position the ends of the leatherleaf fern stems under the flowers. Add enough leatherleaf fern so that the pieces flowing in each direction meet in the middle (Figure 8-8). Place the flower-food packet(s) and care tag at this central joining point. Fold the tissue over the flowers, place the lid on the box and tie a bow around the center of the box.

Figure 8-8. Double-ended rose presentation.

WRAPPING ARRANGEMENTS

Arrangements come in many shapes and sizes, which can sometimes make wrapping them a challenge. Delivery boxes are available in a variety of styles and sizes to help stabilize the bases of tall vases, footed dishes, baskets and bowls. Floral wrap or waxed tissue tucked into these boxes provides added support as well as a decorative flourish. Cellophane (in the form of sheets, rolls or bags) is the wrap of choice for pretty packages while floral wrapping paper provides a more utilitarian wrap for cold weather. The steps that follow detail the procedure for wrapping an arrangement using a roll of cellophane (Figure 8-9).

SUGGESTED MATERIALS

Fresh arrangement

Delivery box

Waxed tissue or floral wrapping paper

Roll of cellophane

Twist tie or chenille stem

3 yards #9-width ribbon

Hand stapler

Figure 8-9. Arrangement wrapped with cellophane.

PACKAGING STEPS

Fold the delivery box according to directions, and staple, if needed.

Position the arrangement container into the box. Stuff waxed tissue or floral wrapping paper around the container, as needed, to provide support.

Measuring Wraps

*To determine the length of cellophane needed, measure the height of the arrangement, and multiply it by 2. Measure the depth of the delivery box, and add that measurement to the first figure. Add 18" - 24" to this figure (the taller the arrangement, the more inches should be added).

For an average arrangement that is 16" tall in a delivery box 6" deep, about 60" of cellophane is needed (16 x 2 = 32 + 6 + 22 = 60).

Lay the cellophane across a table or counter, and position the boxed arrangement in the center. Cut the length of cellophane needed.*

Bring the ends of the cellophane up above the arrangement, and gather the ends together a few inches above the flowers.

PACKAGING STEPS *continued*

Use a twist tie or chenille stem to secure the cellophane at the gathering point. A pouf of cellophane should rise above the twist tie. If the pouf is too large, grasp the top of the pouf, and cut with shears to the desired height.

At the base of the package, on one side of the delivery box, pleat the cellophane as you would the wrapping on the end of a gift box; fold the pleat over itself, and staple.

Align the edges of the cellophane above the stapled pleat, fold the cellophane edge toward the back of the package, and staple several times along the edge to the top.

Repeat Steps 6-7 on the other side of the package.

Tie a piece of ribbon into a bow to conceal the twist tie and add a giftlike finish.

Wrapping Arrangements Variations

I. Plastic or Cellophane Bag

When using a plastic or cellophane bag, follow Steps 1-2 on Page 143, then open up the bag, and gather the sides downward toward the base. Follow the steps shown here.

Place the boxed arrangement into the center of the gathered plastic or cellophane bag.

Carefully pull the bag up over the arrangement, bind with a twist tie, and finish with a satin ribbon bow.

II. Stapled Paper

For a functional package that protects the flowers from weather extremes, follow Steps 1-4 on Page 143, using floral wrapping paper instead of cellophane. Then follow the steps shown here.

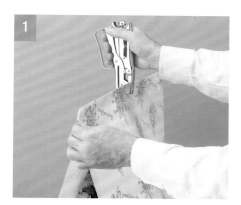

Pull paper up over the design, align the edges, fold the top edges over and staple.

Follow Steps 7-8 on Page 144 to close the sides of the package. Then fold the top corners of the paper, and staple.

III. Flower Tote

For an alternative arrangement wrap with a giftlike appearance, follow Steps 1-2 on Page 143 to stabilize the arrangement. Then, place the delivery box into an oversized plastic (or plastic-lined) flower tote. Gather the handles together, and tie with a coordinating ribbon (Figure 8-10).

Figure 8-10. Arrangement packaged in a plastic tote.

PACKAGING CORSAGES AND BOUTONNIERES

Corsages and boutonnieres are small personal flowers that require special packaging. Though typically packaged individually in boxes designed for this use, several corsages or boutonnieres also can be lined up in rose boxes for occasions such as weddings or banquets. Steps for packaging an individual corsage are provided on Page 146. For boutonnieres, follow the same steps but exchange the corsage wrappings for boutonniere bags, boxes and pins.

SUGGESTED MATERIALS
Corsage
Two corsage pins
Corsage bag and box
Mist bottle
Waxed tissue paper
1-1½ yards #3-width ribbon

PACKAGING STEPS

Add a pin to the corsage by inserting the tip of the pin into the corsage stem on an upward angle. The pin tip should remain within the corsage stem so that it cannot stick anyone handling the design.

Mist the corsage lightly with water, and gently shake off the excess.

Place the corsage into a plastic or cellophane corsage bag, pleat the sides neatly, and fold the end of the bag under. Secure the bag shut with the second corsage pin.

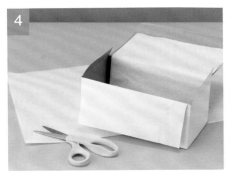

Line the corsage box with a piece of tissue paper trimmed or folded to fit.

Place the bagged corsage inside the box, and fold the tissue over the top.

Close the box, and tie it with a ribbon.

Packaging Corsages and Boutonnieres Variations

I. Packaging When Using an Antitranspirant Spray

Antitranspirants, or finishing sprays, help slow flower deterioration, particularly in designs such as corsages where the flowers no longer have a water source. Lightly mist the flowers with the antitranspirant, and allow the corsage to dry at room temperature. Do not seal flowers that have been treated with an antitranspirant in plastic. Instead, place a bed of orchid grass or shred in the corsage box and lay the flowers on the grass (Figure 8-11).

II. Packaging in Clear Boxes

Clear plastic boxes allow the flowers to be seen without opening the box. When using such a box, place orchid grass or shred in the bottom of the box in place of tissue paper. A corsage bag is optional. Snap the tabs closed on the corsage box to secure the lid, or staple the two layers of plastic together. Tie a decorative ribbon around the box (Figure 8-12).

Figure 8-11. Packaging a corsage misted with an antitranspirant.

Figure 8-12. Packaging a corsage in a clear plastic box.

WRAPPING PLANTS

Wrapping a Plant Pot with Foil

Before sleeving, many plant pots are enhanced with foil or ready-made pot covers. The procedure for using a ready-made pot cover is simple: just drop the plant into the pot-shaped cover. To cover a pot with foil, use one of the procedures that follows.

SUGGESTED MATERIALS

6" potted plant
Florist foil or polyfoil
Floral shears
3½ yards #9-width ribbon
4" or 6" wired wood pick

POT WRAPPING STEPS

Method A: Corner-Folded Cover

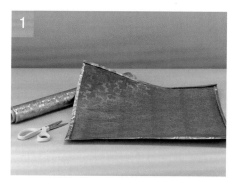

Cut a 20-inch square of double-sided foil. With the color you want outside the pot facing down, fold each edge in approximately ¼". Repeat the ¼" folds a second time to create finished edges. (Note: Complete this step before starting the Pleated Cover as well.)

Place the plant pot in the center of the foil square, and, starting at one corner of the foil, pull the foil upward toward the plant, crimping the foil slightly against the edge of the pot. Pull the foil into neat pleats on either side of the corner, pressing these against the pot and again crimping the foil slightly against the pot's edge.

Continue around the pot, pulling up one corner at a time, continually crimping the foil between one corner and the next.

POT WRAPPING STEPS *continued*

Method B: Pleated Cover

Place the plant pot in the center of the foil square, the edges of which have been folded as in Step 1 for the Corner-Folded Cover on Page 147.

Pull the middle of one side of the foil up the edge of the pot. Grasp the foil along either side of this central point, and fold it into the center to overlap and create a double pleat. Staple the edge where the foil overlaps. Crimp the foil against the edge of the pot.

Repeat Step 2 on the opposite side of the pot. Neatly fold the two remaining edges up against the pot, crimping the foil at the pot's edge and leaving the four corner points collaring the plant.

Method C: "Airplane-Folded" Cover

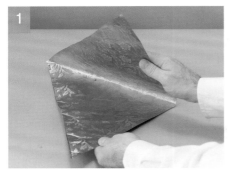

Begin with a 20" square of double-sided foil. Fold the square from one corner to the opposite corner to create a triangle. Fold this triangle in half, matching the tips along its longest edge. Fold this triangle in half again.

With the open edge of the triangle facing up, fold the right edge of the triangle to meet the opposite edge (the triangle's longest side). Repeat this fold one more time.

Encircle the top edge of the pot with a strip of double-sided tape.

Unfold the foil, and place the pot in the center.

Using the folds as a guide and the prepositioned tape to secure it, smooth the foil up against the sides of the pot.

Ribbon Embellishment (can be used to finish method A, B or C)

Insert a wood pick at a slight angle through the foil and into the pot at the point where you want the bow placed. Wrap a length of ribbon around the foil-wrapped pot, bringing the ribbon from midway up the pot's backside and knotting it above the wood pick (with the pick now supporting the ribbon). Trim the ribbon tails to equal lengths.

Create a ribbon bow (according to Steps 1-15 in Chapter III on Pages 45-46), and wire it to another wood pick. Remove the wood pick piercing the pot wrap, and replace it with the wood pick that holds the bow, keeping the knotted ribbon on the backside of this pick. Slide the wood pick all the way into the pot so the bow rests against the container edge.

Fruit and gift baskets are often custom designed by florists. While the process of stacking the items in a gift basket is typically as unique as the components within each, the wrapping procedure is somewhat standard. When cellophane is used, the gift basket is wrapped using the same process as wrapping a fresh flower arrangement (Steps 1-9 on Pages 143 and 144). The only change is the elimination of the delivery box at the base. The procedure that follows is for wrapping a gift basket in shrink film.

WRAPPING STEPS

Cellophane or Shrink Film Over the Top

SUGGESTED MATERIALS

Finished gift basket
Cellophane or shrink film roll or bag
Shrink film heat gun
  (if shrink film is used)

Heat sealer or clear tape
String or twist tie
1 yard #9-width ribbon

Determine wrap measurements following the instructions on Page 143. Cut the cellophane or shrink film, and fold it in half. Form a "bag" using a heat sealer or clear tape to secure the overlapping edges, and place the bag over the basket.

Tie string around the outside of the basket to secure the cellophane or shrink film in place.

Tape down any puckers with clear tape.

Cut off excess cellophane or shrink film.

Tape the cellophane or shrink film to the basket with clear tape.

If shrink film is used, shrink it around the basket with a shrink-film heat gun.

Tape a bow to the top of the basket with clear tape.

Cellophane or Shrink Film Under the Bottom

Place the gift basket on top of the cellophane or shrink film. Pull up the sides and tape into place.

Gather the cellophane or shrink film over the top of the basket, and secure with string or a twist tie.

Trim the pouf. If shrink film is used, shrink it around the basket with a shrink-film heat gun. Avoid the pouf.

Tie a bow underneath the pouf where the film is gathered, to cover the string or twist tie.

Cellophane or Shrink-Film Bag

Place the gift basket inside a cellophane or shrink-film bag.

Fold the sides of the bag close to the basket, and tape in place.

If a shrink-film bag is used, shrink it with a shrink-film heat gun.

Tape a bow to the top of the basket with clear tape.

For cut flowers and foliages to have maximum vase life at the consumer level, it is imperative that they receive proper care during all stages of their journey from farm to florist to consumer. Following are general care and handling procedures for most cut flowers in the flower shop.

Step 1: Sterilize everything. Before flowers arrive, thoroughly wash all flower buckets, cutting tools, and workbenches and countertops with a professional antibacterial bucket cleaner, a kitchen sanitizing spray (similar to ones used to clean countertops) or a solution of one part chlorine bleach and 10 parts water. Repeat this step with every shipment of flowers.

Step 2: Check the shipping temperature. When flowers arrive, immediately check the temperature inside the boxes by inserting the probe of a needle thermometer either through the side of the box, behind the flower heads, or into the water of wet packs. Today, some suppliers are attaching to flower boxes RFID (radio frequency identification) tags, which record the temperature history throughout the shipping process.

If temperatures are higher than 40 F, examine the flowers for insects, foliar or petal diseases, yellowed leaves, and loss of blooms and leaves. Isolate any affected flowers, and contact the supplier.

Step 3: Unpack flower boxes immediately. As you remove flower bunches and inspect them, remove any sleeves and bindings. Leaving sleeves on can help prevent damage to blooms, but the sleeves must be removed eventually to promote air circulation among the flowers. If you can't unpack flowers immediately, store the boxes in a floral cooler at 33 F to 35 F.

Step 4: Clean stems. Remove all leaves that would fall below the water line, and thoroughly rinse stem ends—especially of field-grown flowers—under tepid (100 F to 110 F) running water.

Step 5: Recut stems. Remove at least 1 inch to 3 inches from all stem ends, cutting either under water or in air, with a sharp knife or pruner, to remove dried-out ends and accumulated dirt, debris and microbes in the cells. If cutting flowers under water, change the water (or flower-food solution) *frequently* to prevent it from becoming overly contaminated with bacteria.

Step 6: Place flowers into hydration and/or flower-food solutions. If your flowers *have not* been treated with hydration solution at the grower and/or wholesaler levels, which are the most common treatment points, dip or place the stems into a hydration solution (either an instant dip or a standing solution) immediately upon recutting them.

If your flowers *have* been treated at either or both of these levels, you can forgo this step, if desired, and place your flowers directly into sterilized containers half filled with warm (110 F), *properly proportioned* flower-food solution. (If not mixed to proper concentrations, flower foods can actually promote flower wilting.)

Special formulations: Some flower foods are formulated specifically for certain genera of flowers, such as roses and bulb flowers, as well as for different qualities of water. For example, when bulb flowers are cut, hormone imbalances occur that cause premature leaf yellowing and other problems; therefore, bulb flower foods contain—in addition to the ingredients in standard flower-foods—"replacement" hormones, and they have a lower concentration of sugar, which can aggravate leaf yellowing.

Step 7: Refrigerate the flowers. Place most flowers (except tropical blooms and some bulb flowers) immediately into a *floral cooler* at 33 F to 35 F and 90 percent relative humidity for at least two hours before designing with or selling them. This will allow them time to hydrate.

Tropical flowers require storage temperatures between 50 F and 55 F, and some bulb flowers, such as amaryllises (*Hippeastrums*) and paperwhites (*Narcissi*), prefer temperatures from 36 F to 50 F.

Except for design time, always keep flowers refrigerated until sold or delivered. This will slow their moisture loss, help them maintain their carbohydrate reserves and decrease their sensitivity to ethylene (*see Step 9*).

Sell all flowers within two days of receipt. Flowers held in a floral cooler for more than two days rapidly lose vase life.

Step 8: Monitor your cooler temperature and relative humidity. Check the temperature in your cooler daily by placing a thermometer into a container of water sitting inside the cooler. The water temperature should range from 33 F to 35 F. Check relative humidity with a psychrometer or hygrometer.

Step 9: Protect flowers from ethylene. Purchase only flowers that have been treated with an anti-ethylene compound at the grower or wholesaler levels, at the point of importation or during transportation. In addition, control the amount of ethylene in your store by eliminating sources such as fruit, cigarette smoke, vehicle exhaust and dead flower or plant debris, and using an ethylene filtration system in your cooler. Exposure to ethylene causes flower and bud drop, wilted or prematurely dead blooms, yellow leaves or unopened flowers.

Step 10: Give every walk-in customer, and send with every delivered arrangement, a 10-gram packet of flower food—enough to make one quart of solution. Also provide verbal and written care instructions to every walk-in customer, and send written care instructions with every delivery.

Photos courtesy of Asocolflores; Colombian Association of Flower Exporters; California Cut Flower Commission; Central Florida Fern Co-op; Flower Council of Holland; Quality Growers Floral Company, Inc.; and Veronica Strong *Foliage for Florists*, published by Strong's Greenery.

FLOWER GLOSSARY

Acacia
Mimosa, Silver wattle

Achillea
Fern-leaf yarrow

Achillea
Cottage yarrow,
Milfoil

Aconitum
Monkshood

Agapanthus
African lily,
Lily-of-the-Nile

Allium
Giant *Allium*,
Giant onion

Allium
Round-headed garlic,
Drumstick *Allium*

Alpinia
Ginger

Alstroemeria
Peruvian lily, Inca lily

Ammi
Bishop's weed,
Queen Anne's lace

Anemone
Windflower,
Wind poppy

Anigozanthos
Kangaroo paw

Anthurium
Tail flower,
Flamingo flower

Antirrhinum
Snapdragon

Aster
Heath aster

Aster
New York aster,
Michaelmas daisy

Astilbe
False spiraea, Goat's
beard, Meadow sweet

Banksia

Bouvardia

Bupleurum
Thoroughwax

Callistephus
China aster

Campanula
Canterbury bells

Carthamus
Safflower

Cattleya

Celosia
Cockscomb

Celosia
Feathered amaranth,
Plume *Celosia*

Centaurea
Cornflower,
Bachelor's button

Centaurea
Globe cornflower

Chamelaucium
Waxflower,
Geraldton waxflower

*Chrysanthemum,
Leucanthemum*
Marguerite daisy

153

Convallaria
Lily-of-the-valley

Cosmos
Mexican aster

Craspedia
Billy button

Crocosmia
Montbretia

Cymbidium

Dahlia

Delphinium, Consolida
Larkspur

Delphinium
Belladonna *Delphinium*

Delphinium
Pacific Hybrid
Delphinium

Dendranthema
Incurve chrysanthemum,
Football chrysanthemum

Dendranthema
Spider chrysanthemum,
Fuji chrysanthemum

Dendranthema
Cremone
chrysanthemum

Dendranthema
'Red Rover'
chrysanthemum

Dendranthema
'Garnet King'
chrysanthemum

Dendranthema
Button spray
chrysanthemum

Dendranthema
Cushion spray
chrysanthemum

Dendranthema
Daisy spray
chrysanthemum

Dendranthema
Duet spray
chrysanthemum

Dendranthema
Spider spray
chrysanthemum

Dendrobium

Dianthus
Carnation

Dianthus
Miniature carnation

Dianthus
Sweet William

Echinops
Globe thistle

Erica
Heath, Heather

Eryngium
Sea holly

Freesia

Gardenia
Cape jasmine

Gerbera
Transvaal daisy,
African daisy

Gerbera
Miniature *Gerbera*

Photos courtesy of Ascocolflores; Colombian Association of Flower Exporters; California Cut Flower Commission; Central Florida Fern Co-op; Flower Council of Holland; Quality Growers Floral Company, Inc.; and Veronica Strong Foliage for Florists, published by Strong's Greenery.

Gerbera
Spider *Gerbera*

Gladiolus
Sword lily

Gloriosa
Glory lily

Godetia, Clarkia
Satin flower,
Farewell-to-spring

Gomphrena
Globe amaranth

Gypsophila
Baby's breath

Helianthus
Sunflower

Heliconia
Lobster claw

Heliconia
Parakeet flower

Hippeastrum
Amaryllis,
Barbados lily

Hyacinthus
Hyacinth

Hydrangea

Hypericum
St. John's wort, Tutsan

Iris
Dutch *Iris*, Fleur-de-lis

Lathyrus
Sweet pea

Leptospermum
Tea tree

Leucadendron
'Safari Sunset'
Conebush

Leucospermum
Pincushion

Liatris
Gay-feather, Blazing
star, Button snakeroot

Lilium
Asiatic lily

Lilium
Easter lily,
Bermuda lily

Lilium
L.A. hybrid lily

Lilium
Oriental lily

Limonium
Caspia,
Matted sea lavender

Limonium 'Misty' series
Border sea lavender,
Broad-leaved sea lavender

Limonium
Blue sea lavender,
Seafoam statice

Limonium
Statice, Notch-leaf
statice, Winged statice

Lisianthus, Eustoma
Prairie gentian,
Texas bluebell

Matthiola
Stock, Gillyflower

Moluccella
Bells-of-Ireland

155

FLOWER GLOSSARY

Muscari
Grape hyacinth

Narcissus
Daffodil

Narcissus
Paperwhite

Nerine
Guernsey lily

Ornithogalum
Chincherinchee,
Star-of-Bethlehem

Paeonia
Peony

Paphiopedilum,
Cypripedium
Lady's slipper orchid

Phalaenopsis
Moth orchid

Phlox

Protea
Oleander-leaved *Protea*,
'Pink Mink' *Protea*

Ranunculus
Persian buttercup

Rosa
Garden rose, English
rose, Shrub rose

Rosa
Hybrid tea rose

Rosa
Spray rose

Scabiosa
Pincushion flower,
Scabious

Sedum
Stonecrop

Solidago
Goldenrod

Solidaster
Yellow aster

Stephanotis
Madagascar jasmine

Strelitzia
Bird-of-paradise

Syringa
Lilac

Trachelium
Throatwort

Trachymene, Didiscus
Blue lace flower

Tulipa
Tulip

Tulipa
French tulip

Veronica
Speedwell

Viburnum
Snowball,
Guelder rose

Zantedeschia
Calla, Arum lily

Zantedeschia
Miniature calla,
Miniature arum lily

Zinnia
Youth and old age

156

FOLIAGE GLOSSARY

Photos courtesy of Asocolflores; Colombian Association of Flower Exporters; California Cut Flower Commission; Central Florida Fern Co-op; Flower Council of Holland; Quality Growers Floral Company, Inc.; and Veronica Strong Foliage for Florists, published by Strong's Greenery.

Asparagus
Foxtail fern

Asparagus
Ming fern

Asparagus
Smilax

Asparagus
Sprengeri,
Sprenger fern

Asparagus
Plumosa fern, Lace fern

Asparagus
Tree fern

Buxus
Box, Boxwood,
Oregonia

Camellia

Chamaedorea
Jade palm,
Emerald palm

Cordyline
Ti leaf

Cytisus
Scotch broom

Equisetum
Horsetail, Snake grass

Eucalyptus
Seeded *Eucalyptus*

Eucalyptus
Spiral *Eucalyptus*

Galax
Beetleweed

Gaultheria
Salal, Lemon leaf

Hedera
English ivy

Liriope
Lily grass, Mondo

Magnolia

Monstera
Swiss-cheese plant,
Split-leaf *Philodendron*

Murraya
Orange jasmine,
Coffee

Myrtus
Myrtle

Nephrolepis
Sword fern

Pittosporum
Mock orange,
Japanese mock orange

Pittosporum
Italian *Pittosporum*,
Tawhiwhi, Kohuhu

Ruscus
Butcher's broom, Holland
Ruscus, Israeli *Ruscus*

Ruscus
Italian *Ruscus*

Rumohra, Arachniodes
Leatherleaf fern

Vaccinium
Huckleberry

Xerophyllum
Bear grass

157

INDEX

Anchor pins 9, 15

Balloons 112-121

    Accessories .121

    Air inflation .115

    Balloon "boosters" 116-117

    Balloon bouquets 120-121

    Environmental issues 114

    Helium inflation 115

    Novelty techniques 118-119

    Safety 114

    Sealing 117

    Sizing .115-116

Bouquets (*see "Wedding bouquets"* or *"Balloons: Balloon bouquets"*)

Boutonnieres 49-50

Bows 44-48, 102

Candle mechanics 15

Candy, securing 16-17

Care and handling 152

Chicken wire 9

Corsages .50-57

    Adornments (pearls, beads, jewels) 103

    Corsage pins 103

    Packaging 145-146

    Wrist corsages 55-57

Designs, everyday 18-35

    Bud vases 34

    Oblong centerpiece 27-30

    One-sided triangle 19-22

    Round centerpiece 23-26

    Vase arrangements 31-35

Displays .122-133

    Backgrounds 127-128

    Calendar .132

    Checklist .133

    Principles 128-131

    Props and fixtures 126-127

    Signs 128

    Themes 123-125

Figurines/ceramics, securing 16

Floral foam 7-10, 80

    Cutting 8

    Securing 8-9

    Soaking 7

Flower food 7, 152

Flowers, glossary 153-156

Foam (*see "Floral foam"* or *"Plastic foam"*)

Foliages, glossary 157

Fruit, securing 16-17

Glues/Adhesives 8, 53, 57, 100-101

Greening .11-14

Hair accents 58-61

Packaging 134-151

    Arrangement wrapping 143-145

    Bouquet wrapping 138-140

    Boxed flowers 141-142

    Corsage and boutonniere packaging . .145-146

    Gift basket wrapping 150-151

    Plant-pot wrapping 147-149

    Single flower wrapping 136-137

    Weather 135-136, 140

    Wrapped flowers 138-140

Plastic foam .80

Plush, securing 16

Preservative (*see "Flower food"*)

Stephanotis stems 40

Sympathy designs 62-84

    Basket .63-66

    Casket spray 67-72

    Cross 81-84

    Easel spray 73-76

    Set pieces 80, 84

    Wreath .77-79

Tape .8, 10, 44

    Clear tape .10

    Stem wrap (floral tape) 44

    Waterproof tape 8, 10

Taping flowers and foliages 44, 101

Tulle poufs 48, 105

Vases 10, 31-35

Wedding bouquets 86-111

    Accessories 102-103

    Adornments (pearls, beads, jewels) 103

    Backings 104-106

    Bouquet holders 109-111

    Cascade bouquet 91-94

    Hand-tied bouquet 95-98

    Handles 107-111

    Mechanics 99-101

    Round bouquet 87-90

Wire 37, 101

Wiring chart 42-43

Wiring flowers and foliages 37-43, 101

Wood picks 15, 99-100

Anderson, Gary A. *Floral Design and Marketing*. Columbus, OH: Ohio State University, Ohio Agricultural Education Curriculum Materials Service, 1995.

Basic Floral Design. Lansing, MI: The John Henry Company, 1991.

Bassett, Karey L. *Mechanics of Design*. Southfield, MI: Florists' Transworld Delivery Association, 1994.

burton + Burton education home page. 2006. 29 Dec. 2006 <http://www.burtonandburton.com/education/index.asp>.

Classic Wedding Flowers: Design Handbook. Lansing, MI: The John Henry Company, 2002.

Flowers by Design: Floral Design Basics. Lansing, MI: The John Henry Company, 1998.

"How to Use Hi-Float." Hi-Float home page. 2006. 3 Jan. 2007 <http://www.hifloat.com>.

Hunter, Norah T. *Delmar's Handbook of Flowers, Foliage, and Creative Design*. Albany, NY: Delmar, 2000.

Hunter, Norah T. *The Art of Floral Design*, Second edition. Albany, NY: Delmar, 2000.

John Henry Prom and Homecoming Flowers Tips and Techniques. Lansing, MI: The John Henry Company, 2006.

John Henry Sympathy Flowers Tips and Techniques. Lansing, MI: The John Henry Company, 2005.

Longman, David. *The Instant Guide to Successful House Plants*. New York, NY: Times Books, 1979.

McDaniel, Alan. "R8: Cut Flower Distribution and Handling." *Floral Design Horticulture 2164*. 1999. 18 Dec. 2006 <http://www.hort.vt.edu/faculty/McDaniel/hort2164/LectureText.htm>.

Redbook Florist Services Educational Advisory Committee. *Designing with Balloons and Flowers*, Second edition. Leachville, AR: Redbook Printing Services, 1994.

Redbook Florist Services Educational Advisory Committee. *Purchasing and Handling Fresh Flowers and Foliage*, Second edition. Leachville, AR: Redbook Printing Services, 1994.

Redbook Florist Services Educational Advisory Committee. *Selling and Designing Sympathy Flowers*, Second edition. Leachville, AR: Redbook Printing Services, 1994.

Redbook Florist Services Educational Advisory Committee. *Selling and Designing Wedding Flowers*, Second edition. Leachville, AR: Redbook Printing Services, 1993.

The Guide to Balloons and Ballooning. Ed. Balzer, Mark and Sheena K. Beaverson. 3 Jan. 2007 <http://www.balloonhq.com/faq/>.

Wells, Gary. *Balloons, Flowers and More*. Lansing, MI: The John Henry Company, 1988.

Wright, Michael. *The Complete Indoor Gardener*. New York, NY: Random House, 1974.